EQUILIBRIUM

‹‹‹‹‹ ›››››

EQUILIBRIUM

⋘ ⋙
Spirituality for Everyday People

JO WORSFOLD

First published in 2019 by JPW Publishing
ABN 85 933 435 740
lumanova.com.au

Copyright © Jo-Anne Worsfold, 2019

All rights reserved. No part of this publication may be reproduced or transmitted in any form, or by any means, electronic or mechanical, including photocopying, recording, or any information storage or retrieval system, without prior permission in writing from the author.

Every reasonable effort has been made to trace copyright holders of material reproduced in this book, but if any have been inadvertently overlooked, or acknowledged incorrectly, the author would be glad to hear from them so appropriate changes can be made to reprints.

Cover photography Mel De Ruyter @ Melanie Kate Photography
Typesetting Jo Worsfold @ JPW Publishing
Cover design Melanie Kate Photography and JPW Publishing

A catalogue record for this book is available from the National Library of Australia

ISBN 978 0 6487083 1 5 (pback)
ISBN 978 0 6487083 0 8 (ebook)

To borrow this book from your local library, contact your library directly to recommend they stock this title.

Disclaimer
The author is not affiliated with any of the corporate or third-party entities or individuals mentioned in or involved in the distribution of this work. The material in this book is of the nature of general comment only and does not represent professional advice. This book is distributed and sold under the understanding that the author is not engaged in rendering professional medical services. To the maximum extent permitted by law, no responsibility for loss caused to any individual or organization acting on or refraining from action as a result of the material in this publication can be accepted by the publisher or the author.

Some names and characteristics within this book have been changed to protect privacy.

The papers used in the manufacture of this book are sustainably sourced, in line with the printer's paper sourcing guidelines and sustainability practices.

Dedicated to Alicia and Ethan.

*'Live your own truth.
Be authentically genuinely you,
then watch as happiness finds you.'*
- Jo Worsfold, Spiritualist and Healing Channel

CONTENTS

Introduction	xiii

PART I MY STORY

Chapter 1. A Fresh Start: The Escape	2
Chapter 2. A Fresh Start: Still Running	7
Chapter 3. Coming Home, To Myself	19
Chapter 4. Heal, Love, Learn	25

PART II THE NITTY GRITTY

Chapter 5. Spiritual Energy: What Is It, Really?	40
Soul Energy	41
Auras	45
Chakras	47
Earth Energy	49
Universal Energy	50
Chapter 6. The Synergy of Spiritual Energy	53
Communication of Spiritual Energy	54
Energetic Frequencies	56
Spiritual Energy and Death	57
Chapter 7. Intuition	61
The Yes / No Test	61
Pendulums	64
The Sway Test	65
Keeping it Real	68
Chapter 8. Love	71
Loving You	72
Practicing Self-Love	74
The 'I Love Me' Mantra	75
Loving Your Body	76
Self-Love Through Instinct and Skill	78
Sharing the Love	79

    Love and Anger / Conflict   80
    The Joy List   84

Chapter 9. Ego   85

Chapter 10. Lifestyle Balance: Choices and Change   89
    Belinda's Story   90
    Choices and Intuition   94
    Tools for Change   95
        Vision Boards   95
        Positive Affirmations   100
    Other Ways to Bring About Change   103
    The Importance of Lifestyle Balance   104
    Letting Go of the Past   105

Chapter 11. Lessons: Navigating Through the Speed Bumps   108

Chapter 12. 'Dear Human, With Love'   115

Chapter 13. Miracles   118
    My Health Miracle   119
    Dad's Ring Miracle   126
    Miracles of All Shapes and Sizes   128

Chapter 14. Making a Difference   130

PART III SELF-CARE: YOUR TURN

Chapter 15. Meditation   138
    Breathing Meditation   139

Chapter 16. Spiritual Healers Aplenty   144
    The Role of the Healer   145
    Reiki   146
    Aboriginal Healing   150
        Aboriginal On Country Healing   152
    Shamanic Healing   156
    Crystal Healing   160
        Cleanse Your Crystals   162
    Be Your Own Healer   163
        Self-Healing   163
        The Healing Power of Words ('Love Thyself')   166

Chapter 17. Energy Medicine   170

Tapping	170
Tapping Sequence	173
Acupuncture	176
Acupressure Exercise	179
Grounding or Earthing	180
Earthing Visualisation Exercise	181
Cleanse Your Energy	182
Shower Cleanse Exercise	182
Strengthen Your Energy	183
Protect Your Energy	183
Bubble Machine Exercise	184
Holistic Medicine	185
Chapter 18. Nutrition and Fitness of the Mind and Body	**188**
The Food Disasters	190
Intuition and Food	193
Energy and Food	196
Herbs, Beautiful Herbs	198
Intuition and a Happy Body	200
The Great and Powerful Mind	203
Mindfulness Activities	204
Chapter 19. Other Practical Tips and Tricks	**206**
Massage	206
Kahuna Massage	207
Abhyanga (including Abhyanga Self-Massage)	208
Foot, Abdominal and Ear Massages	211
Clinical Hypnotherapy	213
Autosuggestion	215
Bath Time	218
Space Clearing	220
The Five Senses	224
Chapter 20. Manifestation of Your Dreams	**227**

PART IV COMING FULL CIRCLE

Chapter 21. Your Soul Speaks	237
Chapter 22. The Everyday You	240
Chapter 23. Guidance from Spirit	245

⋘ INTRODUCTION ⋙

I have a memory from when I was a very young girl, perhaps five or six years old. I was sitting in the back seat of our family wagon, gazing out the window as we made our way to my aunty and uncle's new house. I had not been to this house before; in fact I hadn't been in this part of town before. I watched the houses moving past my window, one after the other.

We turned a corner and on this next road the rugged natural landscape was all around us, dwarfing our little vehicle. This road took a huge, sweeping arc all the way around a small body of water. I remember the road was quite elevated; to my young eyes, it felt like we were driving around the top of a big, circular dam.

I was overcome with a feeling of familiarity. I knew this place! Suddenly, it was just me and this place – me and these surroundings. Everything else – the car, my family – had all become a blurry outline.

Driving around that sweeping road took only a minute or two, but to me, it took an eternity because time stood still. My eyes, wide with wonder, urgently searched the landscape for an explanation. *How did I know this place?*

PART I

MY STORY

1

A FRESH START: THE ESCAPE

'I was terrified and exhilarated at the thought of starting over.'

It has taken me many long, soul-searching years to come to terms with the choices made and the actions taken when I was a young adult, having just moved out of my family home and muddling my way through the big, wide world of independence. Back then, I only saw the world and everyone in it as one-dimensional. And back then, to me, the term *soul searching* was some fluffy, overused cliché.

Now, this same phrase has taken on a whole new meaning for me. Soul searching: discovering what it is that makes me truly happy. Making peace with my mistakes. Unlocking gifts that have, for years, gone unnoticed or ignored. Finding an inner strength to express deep emotions and desires and opinions that have previously been masked by the desire to please others. Discovering the wondrous world of energy; of the Universe. Learning lessons. Finding happiness. Finding love. Finding home.

At the age of twenty-one, I moved from my quiet little home town in Tasmania to the city of Perth, Western Australia. I was young, with no commitments and desperately keen to see what the rest of Australia had to offer. I was terrified and exhilarated at the thought of starting over. I was going West to make a better life for myself; a new job, new friends, new adventures, new romance. I was also going West to escape past failed relationships and was perhaps even trying to escape myself. A few too many bad choices later, I needed to start afresh.

So, much to the dismay of my beautiful and loving parents, I sold most of my humble belongings at local markets, packed the few remaining essentials I would need to take with me on my adventure, and bought myself a one-way plane ticket West.

I was invited to live with a friend of a friend, and the two of us quickly transitioned from roommates to best friends. Jess was like a breath of fresh air; she was carefree, funny and outgoing and I couldn't believe I was lucky enough to be living with her and calling her my friend. Life in Tasmania, it seemed, had been left for dust.

I was a new person, with new friends, a new car and a new job. I was absolutely adamant I wouldn't make the same stupid mistakes I made in Tassie, which pretty much involved wasting all my money on meaningless possessions and hooking up with meaningless men and having destructive, meaningless, sort of, not quite there (despite my best efforts), half-arsed relationships. No! I would no longer allow myself to be a disposable and interchangeable gap-filler with no value. No one in Perth knew me or my past and I was more than happy to keep it that way.

The house Jess and I lived in was an old, solid double brick house with a below ground pool, a big garage and a huge back yard and it was really cheap rent. This was our party house, where we had so many good times and very few bad times. My life was so easy now! In our yard stood a grand old orange tree, so we were fortunate to be able to pick and eat an abundance of delicious, sweet oranges every year. Even now, twenty years on, whenever I eat an orange, I think of my party house in Perth.

My younger sister came over from Tasmania to live with us, as well as occasional fourth renters who would come and go as the months drifted by. It was a very busy house!

The next couple of years of my life were spent working hard at my new job which I loved, building new friendships, crazy-fun house parties, loud concerts, swimming in our pool in forty-degree heat in the middle of a Perth summer, and a whole lot of road tripping around WA.

I finally felt like I had a handle on my new-found independence; it was helping me figure out who I was and what I was passionate about. I was finding my confidence again, as memories of my past slowly drifted into the back recesses of my mind.

There was a rumour of a ghost in our share house; the ghost of an elderly man who lived there and had passed away many years ago. Perhaps, the ghost of the man who planted our orange tree. I had heard stories of people seeing his ghost sitting on the brick wall at the front of our house.

I didn't believe in ghosts back then; I just couldn't fathom how something like that could exist. I was a very logical thinker, and the idea of ghosts defied all my logic. I mean, if I can't see it with my eyes or touch it with my body then it simply doesn't exist. Pretty straight forward and reasonable, right?

And maybe, if I'm being completely honest, ghosts did scare me just a wee little bit. I'd never heard of ghosts being anything other than a supernatural phenomenon that nightmares are made of. Which could explain why I never wanted to move into the bedroom at the front of our house, overlooking the brick wall.

Okay, I admit it, ghosts gave me the creeps. But surely, they weren't real, were they?

At that stage of my life, I didn't give a lot of thought to what happens when a person dies. I think somewhere deep down I had hoped that death didn't mean the end, but I never lent any headspace to the idea, so I never explored my feelings on death, ghosts, the afterlife and all that other wonderful, spiritual stuff. I hadn't been around death a great deal growing up.

I lost my grandparents when I was still quite young and all I can remember from their passing is feelings of confusion, because I didn't understand death at that young age. I also remember feelings of sadness, as I watched my parents grieve for their loved ones. But I never questioned death itself.

As a young teenager in high school, I would push the glass in a séance and swear black and blue that I didn't do it. I just didn't – couldn't – believe in any of it, and I was always thoroughly entertained as I watched my friends all scream with fear and delight as the glass moved across the Ouija board. I was bored with waiting for *something* to move the glass and wanted to liven up our sleepovers.

My friends always accused me of pushing the glass and I always vehemently denied it – this was serious ghostly stuff, I wouldn't dare push the glass! We would always go to so much effort to make a Ouija board out of paper, studiously writing out each letter of the alphabet, then arranging all the letters on our handmade board so the ghosts could talk to us.

The idea of ghosts was a scary concept for thirteen-year-old me, who also happened to be terrified of the dark and of being alone. If I made fun of ghosts, I didn't feel threatened by them. If I pushed the glass, a ghost would not be given the opportunity to do so.

There's no such thing as ghosts, there's no such thing as ghosts.

One hot Saturday morning, wearing very little clothing – thanks to the scorching heat – I was doing my share of the weekly chores in my rental house in the West. I was vacuuming the lounge room carpet, when a gentle, loving, but firm hand touched my back between my bare shoulder blades. There was only myself and Jess home that morning, and I knew Jess had plans to head out for the day, so I assumed the hand on my back was her way of getting my attention to say goodbye. I turned, expecting to see my bestie standing there with a big smile on her face, ready to say she was heading off. But there was no one standing behind me.

This took me by surprise – I had just felt someone's hand on my back! It was warm to the touch, and I could even recall the outline of the hand and the fingers all touching my skin. I called Jess's name, and she didn't respond. I walked through the whole house looking for Jess, but she had already gone for the day and the house was empty. I wasn't feeling afraid or uneasy; the touch I felt was too loving and genuine for me to fear it. But I was very confused!

Later that day, I told Jess about the events of my morning. She was very intrigued and asked me lots of questions and all we could put it down to was that, just maybe, it was the ghost of the old deceased man saying hello. I wasn't entirely convinced, but at the same time I didn't know how else to explain the hand I felt on my back. One thing I knew was certain though, if *that* was a ghost, he wasn't scary. Not even one little bit.

2

A FRESH START: STILL RUNNING

'My own fear kept it at bay, just a little longer.'

After two years of living in Perth, I moved to the Pilbara in Western Australia. The Pilbara is a beautiful region in northern Western Australia that is abundant in ancient landscapes, mining towns, pristine coastlines and red earth. I wanted to work in the mines so I could afford to travel; I wanted to see more of my beautiful country and have life-changing experiences in every state. I also wanted to escape from those self-destructive patterns that seemed to have, most annoyingly, followed me from Tassie to WA.

I thought leaving Tassie would be my silver lining. But a person can't run away from themselves. And it seemed that lessons still hadn't been learned. I had subtly slipped back to old habits of chasing men who had no respect for me whatsoever and spending all my money recklessly and excessively. I had regressed to that familiar self-loathing state of despair. I was fruitlessly searching for fulfilment and happiness and self-worth. I was miserable again. I hated myself. And I wanted to escape, again.

My relocation to the Pilbara happened so much faster than I anticipated. Everything fell into place and before I knew it, I was on a plane and headed to Newman, a bustling little mining town in the middle of the Pilbara.

I landed a job with a mining company working as an Office Administrator. Living and working in remote WA was a far cry from life in Tasmania. I remember, when I first arrived, being in awe of the landscape and the people of this region; it was new and exciting and I had high hopes for a future full of adventure.

One of my responsibilities as the Site Administrator was the daily town run. I would drive from the mine site to the middle of town to pick up lunches for the office crew, I would also go to the bank and do a few other chores.

One day, I had finished all my chores in town and was now driving my boss' Toyota Landcruiser along the gravelly red-dirt-ridden dusty access road back to site. The radio was playing some random song from the local radio station quietly in the background. I was concentrating intently on the road because, although I did enjoy the daily drive, I was never a big fan of driving on unsealed roads.

I knew this road like the back of my hand; I drove along it at least three times a day and I knew every bend and bump well. As I came around yet another bend in the big red track, I saw a car approaching me. It was an old yellow sedan and the driver was leaving the mine site, driving along the access road and heading back to town. Nothing unusual or alarming happened as we passed each other on that gravel road. I thought I recognised the driver, but wasn't certain because I barely gave him a glance as we passed each other. I was too busy concentrating on the gravel surface I was driving on.

A split second after that car passed me, I saw a scene unfold in my mind. I saw that little yellow car lose control on the gravel and roll a couple of times, landing in the scrub on the side of the road. That scene took barely a second to play out in my mind, but it was so vivid. It was like witnessing a flicker of a scene from a movie playing in my head and I was, for a split second, taken away from driving the Landcruiser and transported somewhere else and before I even knew what had happened, I was back in the Landcruiser, heading to the mine.

It gave me cold chills. I glanced in my rearview mirror and breathed a sigh of relief as I watched the yellow car travelling safely off in the distance. I continued my drive back to the mine site, and although I had dismissed that terrifying scene in my head, I couldn't shake the uneasy feeling settling in. A favourite song of mine then came on the radio, and this was enough to distract me from my uneasy thoughts for a while.

As I approached the carpark in front of the site offices, I slowed the Landcruiser to a crawl to accommodate the chaos that was greeting me. My stomach lurched. There were people scrambling in all directions; some running for their vehicles, some running in and out of the offices in a panic, almost all of them on their two-way radios shouting instructions to others who were elsewhere in the mine. Oh my god. What was happening?

I parked up and flew out of the vehicle, towards the chaos. I was shaking. No, I was trembling. My body was a mass of visibly trembling fear. I could barely walk or speak. I managed to squeak out something incoherent that should have resembled, 'What's happened? What's going on?' but everyone else was in such a mad panic, they either didn't hear my pathetic squeaks of enquiry or they didn't have the time to answer. This panicked me even further.

I ran inside the site office to find just as much chaos in there as in the carpark. Doors being slammed. People yelling at other people. Everyone pulsing through the office like shooting stars that couldn't get to where they were going fast enough.

'Please! What's happened?' I begged.

I needed someone to tell me what was going on, but I actually already knew.

I knew that little yellow car had rolled on the gravel access road. What I didn't know, was whether the driver had been injured, or worse. My mind was beginning to shut down on me. In fact, my entire body was losing its ability to perform simple functions like, say, standing upright.

I managed to corner a couple of the site managers in the office and demanded to be told what was going on. By this stage, my legs were almost crumpling beneath me, as I struggled to muster the strength to keep it together and stay upright. One of them glanced at me, then did a double take as he noticed my distressed condition. He told me there had been a car roll over on the access road.

'It was a yellow car, wasn't it?' I asked him.

He assumed I had witnessed the accident but he was wrong; I didn't see it happen – not with my eyes, anyway. He couldn't understand why I was so upset and I didn't know how to explain to him what I had *seen* earlier. I also didn't know why my body was reacting this way. Clearly, I had gone into shock, but I didn't know that at the time.

Thankfully, the driver of the vehicle was unharmed. Yes, the car had lost control in the gravel and had rolled a couple of times; my vision was spot on. And I was freaking out over it. I didn't understand what had just happened to me and this frightened me something fierce.

Thank god the driver of that yellow car escaped uninjured. Thank god. Thank god. Thank god. That was one of the things that kept echoing through my mind, as my senses started to return. Had anything happened to that driver, I would have ended up in hospital right alongside him from the shock that was threatening to consume me.

I spent much of the rest of that day in an unfocused and surreal state. I never did try and explain to anyone why I was so upset that day and how I knew what had happened to that little yellow car. And thank goodness no one ever asked me. I was convinced they would all think I had lost my mind, because that is exactly what I was thinking.

I now know that my vision of that little yellow car was me bearing witness to my soul beginning to transform. It was the Universe, in its infinite wisdom, deciding it was time for me to connect on a deeper level to the incredibly vast and wondrous universal energy that is constantly flowing in and around us all.

I was shown a peek of my true potential, but for whatever reason, it just wasn't time for me to embrace my true potential with open arms. My own fear kept it at bay, just a little longer. This was, however, a very significant moment in my life that will forever stay with me. At the time, it made no sense to me and frightened me to my core. Now, I see it for what it was – a fleeting moment of total connectedness to the energy in and around me.

It was in this little town called Newman where I met my future husband. We started dating and within a couple of years we were married and had moved further north from Newman to the sleepy coastal town of Point Samson. Over the coming years, I would wrestle with thoughts such as: *What does he see in me? Does he really love me? I'm not good enough, pretty enough, funny enough.*

That internal voice in my head was having a lovely time planting toxic seeds of self-destruction inside me. It was having a grand old time keeping me in emotional chains with its hurtful, soul-destroying narrative.

You must understand, this was all internal dialogue. To others,

I appeared happy and in control of my life. After all, I had a loving husband who adored me and we were planning to start a family. We had our ups and downs, but overall, things were great. We had plenty of money. We had great jobs. My life, on the surface, was perfect and there were many moments of happiness and lots of fun. But that pesky internal voice inside me kept gnawing away until I feared there would be nothing left.

I fell pregnant a few weeks before we were due to be married and, although we didn't expect to conceive a baby quite so soon, we were both thrilled and so excited about our future family. I was having a baby! We had it all mapped out, the wedding, honeymoon, pregnancy, birth of our first-born child. It was going to be a glorious year!

However, three days before our wedding, I miscarried. Our bubble of family bliss was obliterated in the blink of an eye – I was free-falling into despair, and I had a wedding to get through in just three days' time. There was no time to grieve, and no one to talk to about it because no one even knew we were pregnant – we were going to surprise everyone after our honeymoon with the news.

My husband was much stronger than me. He told me we'd try again. He told me we had each other, and we'd be fine. It was his strength that got me through those next few days. Thankfully, on my wedding day all thoughts of my lost child were left behind and I was able to enjoy one of the happiest days of my life. It was like someone hit the pause button on my grief, so I could at least participate in my precious wedding day, then as soon as the sun set over the ocean that evening, they hit the play button again. Losing a child I have never met is complicated. I don't know them, I've only known of them for a few short weeks, yet I love them anyway. And I am shattered by their loss.

The doctor told us that early miscarriage is more common than we realise and not to worry. We picked ourselves up, dusted ourselves off, and we tried again. Almost immediately, we were pregnant with baby number two. This pregnancy lasted only a fraction longer than the first, before I miscarried again.

Thump.

Crashed again.

Those few months were an insane rollercoaster of emotions; the highest of the highs, then the lowest of the lows. The pendulum was swinging hard and fast and I was sick to my stomach from the motion of my life.

As I lay in a hospital bed, two days after the second miscarriage, I was recapping the horrendous events of that day when more self-destructive thoughts seeped in: *Was it my fault? I shouldn't have done the gardening that day and overexerted myself! Was there something wrong with my body? What the hell was wrong with me?*

Earlier that day I appeared physically fine and had the all clear from my doctor, but my mood was very low. My husband suggested I drive myself to Karratha for a shopping day to cheer myself up. It was an easy thirty-minute drive to a neighbouring town on the coast. He said moping on the couch for days on end was not doing me any favours. He knows me well and knew that a day at the shops would lift my spirits. He was right! It started out as a really fun day, and then things went horribly wrong.

One minute, I'm happily ambling through the shopping centre with my bags of newly purchased clothes swinging from my arms. My long, flowy, cheesecloth skirt swooshed past my ankles as I strolled along without a care in the world. My dose of retail therapy had done the trick.

Then a strange feeling of letting go, deep in my pelvis, pulled me up in my tracks and I felt a trickle of warmness tickle my thighs. I realise I must have started menstruating, so I made a dash to the public toilet. In the tiny cubicle, made even smaller by the mountains of shopping bags all around me, I lifted my skirt and pulled down my underwear to see if my suspicions were correct. I collapsed on the toilet from the sight of the blood furiously flowing from the depths of my pelvis. I waited for it to subside.

It didn't.

The sound of the blood pouring into the toilet sounded just like someone pouring a jug of water into the toilet bowl. A jug of water that was never ending. It didn't stop, or even subside. My mind began racing with options: I couldn't call my husband because he was at least a forty-five-minute drive away and I didn't have any other family nearby to call.

I sat and I waited for what seemed like an eternity in that confined, suffocatingly small cubicle. The blood kept coming. I decided I had to get to hospital, and fast. I knew if I waited for someone to come to me, I would be in trouble.

Adrenaline kicked in and I sprang into action. I unravelled massive fist-sized wads of toilet paper from the roll on the wall and stuffed it firmly in between my legs. I tied my long skirt up underneath me, nappy-like, hoping it would catch the torrents of bright red, and I grabbed my bags and moved quickly but cautiously to my car. Driving to the hospital, with adrenaline coursing through my body, the only thing going through my mind was: *Please don't let me die. Please don't let me die.*

I was all alone.

I'm now running down the empty corridor of the hospital, trying to find someone – *anyone* – to help me. I find a lone nurse sitting at a station and she politely asks me how she can help.

'Help me – I'm bleeding,' I stammered. I don't know what else to say – my words are catching in my throat. Confused, the nurse follows my gaze down to my groin. Realisation spreads across her face and she springs to action, grabbing a wheelchair and bringing it to me. Finally, I feel safe.

Finally, I can stop being strong and brave; my survival instincts and actions are no longer needed. I simultaneously collapse into the chair and begin to moan. It rises in my chest and throat like a brute force. The sobs explode from me, as the nurse races me down the hall to find a doctor.

I awaken after the dilation and curettage medical procedure; the doctors had to 'clean me out' after the miscarriage. Somehow, my husband found out (did I call him? I'm not certain) and he was there with me, holding my hand. I had lost a lot of blood. I was exhausted. I was defeated. I was empty.

My husband was so positive, he was my rock and he took perfect care of me. He kept his chin up and he kept on going. I tried. Truly, I did. But the best I could do was get from one day to the next, wallowing in grief over the loss of my babies and wallowing in frustration at myself for being so incompetent. My mood swings became a regular part of my day – bless my husband for putting up with me.

I wanted to know what was going on with my body. I felt like I had lost all control and had no say in how my body behaved. I felt so disconnected from myself and I wanted to fix it. I heard through the small-town grapevine, of a lady in the area who offered alternative medical services and she had an excellent reputation. One of the services she offered was Bowen Therapy and although I had never heard of Bowen before, I was intrigued and keen to give it a go.

I arrived at the Bowen Therapist's treatment rooms and told her my story. I lay down on the therapy table feeling quite anxious and wondered if I was doing the right thing. But as soon as she lay her hands on me, the anxiety vanished.

Waves of relaxation washed through my entire body, quickly sending me into a peaceful and dreamless sleep. I don't know how long the session went for. I had no idea what she had done to me!

I remember waking in the room and feeling like I had been in a very deep sleep for a very long time. I felt rested. And I felt different, somehow. She told me as I was leaving that she didn't think I would need a second appointment, and she was right.

Take three! We have conceived a baby. We reach week twelve. We reach week twenty, then week thirty, then the due date is here! Finally, I give birth to our baby girl, Alicia Grace. She is everything we could have hoped for, and then some. This perfect, tiny, wrinkled little bundle of cuteness is all ours. All the trauma and heartache from the past year or so suddenly doesn't matter anymore. We finally have the family we have been wishing for.

Life was amazing! Being a mum is what I was born to do. I adore every second of every day with my baby girl and my doting husband. I have never for one second doubted my ability as a mother or doubted my daughter's love for me. It was having my daughter in my life that made me realise I *did* have a chance of overcoming all my worries and insecurities regarding my relationship with my husband – worries which I had now learned to live with, to tolerate, like an irritating but familiar acquaintance, and that one day I could perhaps let go of my past and finally be free. My daughter gave me hope.

We decided our daughter should have a brother or sister who is close to her in age, so as soon as I am physically able we are trying for baby number two. I was destined for one more heart-breaking miscarriage, before we were blessed with the healthy pregnancy and safe arrival of our beautiful, funny and affectionate baby boy, Ethan John. We now have our pigeon-pair; our two little monkeys.

Ethan was born in Perth, Western Australia. After Alicia was born, we moved from the Pilbara back to Perth to be closer to family and to find a place that really felt like home. I still wanted to shed my past and quieten the nagging and negative voices in my head, but there was little time for myself with a newborn and a toddler to care for. So I kept on moving forward, one foot in front of the other, one day at a time.

I believe that Ethan was sent to teach me. From day one, he has had me on my toes. He has made me question everything I thought I knew about motherhood and babies. He had poor health right from the start; he contracted a virus that stopped him breathing at just a couple of weeks old, he was lactose-intolerant from birth, and he had what doctors diagnosed as 'colic' – he was irritable, unsettled and unhappy *a lot.*

This all encouraged me to think outside the box. I was determined to find out why my baby boy was not a happy baby and as always, I was taking a holistic approach. I began seeking the help of not only general practitioners and paediatricians whom I trusted, but also naturopaths and other alternative therapists.

It was around this time that I sunk into a very deep state of postnatal depression and anxiety. All the stresses and trauma of my life had caught up with me. I had two beautiful babies under two-years-old, I had a loving and supportive husband who, on a side note, was also going through his own stuff – working on facing his past and making peace with it.

I would have done anything for my family – moved mountains, as they say. But I couldn't have given two damns about myself. I ate fast food every single day. I binged on chocolate every day, several times a day. I couldn't stand to look at myself in the mirror. My hair was falling out, to the extent that I had noticeable bald patches all over my scalp. Eczema was covering most of my body. I felt fat and bloated. I didn't think my husband loved me. It. Was. Shit. But I kept on moving through the days, one day at a time. One foot in front of the other. Like a lifeless, soul-less robot.

My husband desperately wanted to help me – he wanted his wife back. He see-sawed between sadness, frustration and anger. We fought a lot. But we kept moving forward one day at a time, one foot in front of the other.

We decided we needed a change, and fast, so we sold our house in Perth, sold most of our belongings and we moved our family to Tasmania. I was going home.

3

COMING HOME, TO MYSELF

'Mere seconds stood between feeling burdened by jagged memories to feeling free.'

In 2009, eleven years after I left my home state, I returned to live in Tasmania with my husband and our two young children. In the years that followed, I learned to see the world in an entirely new way. My eyes, my heart and my mind have been opened to possibilities and concepts I never thought fathomable. Since that move in 2009 my life, my health and my happiness have all dramatically improved. I am now blessed with a beautiful family *and* a happy life. I am now deeply, wholeheartedly happy! Hooray!

However even when life is this great, there are still hurdles to face. But I'm okay with the hurdles because I now realise they are life lessons. Every single one of them. One of the repetitive hurdles I have endured over the years is my chronic, niggly health problems and although this has cost my family and I tens of thousands of dollars and hours upon hours upon *hours* of my time spent researching possible causes and cures, it taught me one of the most valuable lessons I have ever learned: trust in myself, and in the Universe, and I will find happiness. My health complaints are also what led me to energy healing, and to everything contained within this book. Everything happens for a reason.

Over the years, I tried everything possible to help rid me of my constantly flaring eczema, bloated stomach, anxiety, borderline depression, food addiction, eating disorder, and other debilitating symptoms. I never once for a single second thought these symptoms were normal and something I had to learn to live with, despite what many other well-meaning people told me over the years. I knew, in my heart of hearts, there was a reason *why* my body and mind weren't consistently happy and healthy.

I persisted with Western Medicine, I also took a holistic approach and tried countless naturopaths and other alternative healing modalities. All seemed to help for a short time but the symptoms soon returned and sometimes, they returned with a vengeance. I was learning so much, yet was unable to fix myself.

I was feeling deflated, defeated and angry. Why couldn't I figure out what was wrong with me? No one seemed to know – they were all guessing, to a certain extent. I kept hearing of other people who were curing themselves of all sorts of symptoms by eating a certain diet, taking a certain supplement or drug, undergoing a certain procedure or therapy and this frustrated me even more because nothing was working long term for me. So where was I going wrong?

One day, while making conversation with a yoga instructor who taught one of the first classes I ever attended, I confided in her my constant health struggles. She suggested I pay a visit to a local naturopath whom I had never heard of before. 'You need to have an open mind, this lady works like no other. She can tell you what is wrong with your body, just by touching your hand,' she said.

Later that day I called the naturopath who magically diagnoses with the touch of her hand, and I was able to make an appointment with her for the following week. That appointment was the start of my spiritual awakening.

At that first appointment, watching her work was captivating and confusing. She lay her hand on mine and proceeded to work her way through a pre-made checklist, busily ticking off items and making short notes on her sheet of paper. She then lay me on a lounge and proceeded to tap my forehead as she quietly whispered words. She wasn't talking to me though, and I had no idea who she was talking to or what she was saying. I left there feeling very different to when I first walked in – lighter, somehow. Despite this lady being draped in mystery, I knew I had found the person who could help me kick start my healing journey.

I booked an appointment for my young son to see her and she worked through the same process with him. He was so relaxed that he fell into a deep sleep on her lounge – something very out of character for him. She quietly chanted her mysterious words, as she gently tapped his forehead.

As she was working her magic on my son, she looked over at me. I was sitting there on the other side of the room, completely engrossed in watching her work. I was in awe of this lady, and I had a million and one questions running through my mind. I wanted to desperately pull her aside and have her tell me everything. As she looked at me, sitting on the other side of the room, a big grin spread across her face. 'You're hungry to know more, aren't you?' she says.

I was a bit taken aback by her question, so I just smiled nervously and politely and nodded eagerly. I didn't want to interrupt my son's healing. She never mentioned it again, and neither did I. Although I didn't have many appointments with her, this brief encounter was enough to make me question everything I thought I already knew and believed in. And I was determined to learn more.

I couldn't get the mysterious naturopath out of my mind. In the coming weeks, I caught up with an old high school friend and found myself telling her all about my surreal experiences. She put me in touch with another lady who she was certain could answer my many questions. This is how I met the lady who changed my life forever.

Florence is an eighty-year-old Reiki Master and from my very first phone call with Florie, I was hooked. She spoke of souls, the Universe, and of negative and positive energy. She was so matter of fact and confident when she spoke and by the time I hung up the phone, my head was buzzing with all this delicious new knowledge. These ideas and beliefs were so foreign to me but somehow it all made sense.

The next thing I knew, I was booked to attend a weekend-long Reiki Attunement and Spiritual Retreat, hosted by Florie. I was determined to heal myself and let go of my past, once and for all.

It is difficult to find the words to describe what I experienced and how I felt during that weekend away with Florie. There was a small group of us, all from different parts of Tasmania, and Florie led us through so many activities such as drumming – using the vibrations from the drums to realign and heal our bodies' energies, tarot and oracle card readings – interpreting the messages Spirit was communicating with us through the various messages and images on the cards, experimenting with gemstones and crystals – feeling their energy and experiencing first-hand what they have to offer us.

There is a particular experience from that weekend I will never forget. We were all in the living room, casually swapping stories while drinking hot cups of sweet, freshly brewed tea. There was a beautiful energy filling the room, enveloping us all as we got to know each other. I was loving every second yet feeling completely out of my depth at the same time. I had never heard a group of people talk about the things they were discussing that afternoon.

The questions kept pouring from my lips as my hunger to learn more intensified. I wasn't sure if I believed what they were saying but my goodness it was fascinating to listen to! I was in the middle of a particularly deep conversation with a lady, talking about love and relationships. Mid-conversation, she stood and silently walked towards me. Without saying a word, she placed her hands on me – one hand on my chest and the other on my back between my shoulder blades.

The reaction was instant: piercing feelings of grief, betrayal and loss shot straight through my core. The tears sprang from my eyes without warning. *Oh, those tears.* They ran down my face, down my neck, down my chest, caressing my skin with their salty dampness. Still, not a single word was spoken. She just smiled kindly at me, as she continued to lovingly but firmly hold her hands on my body until the piercing pain and the tears subsided.

In just a few short seconds I felt like the weight of twenty-years-worth of lost love and painful memories had been expelled from my soul. Mere seconds stood between feeling burdened by jagged memories to feeling free.

Her magic had taken hold of me with its fiercely loving hands and I was left breathless and confused. I was utterly exhausted. I collapsed in a pile of relief on the lounge, and then she held me. She gently stroked my hair and whispered in my ear that everything was going to be alright. She comforted me back to the now – back to that intimate gathering in the living area where everyone was still happily chatting and sipping tea.

I felt like time had stood still for those few moments, and as I gazed around the room taking in my surroundings and finding my bearings, everything looked different. All the colours and textures in the room were brighter. The hum of voices sounded sweet and crisp to my ears. I felt like I could float away, light as a feather, off that lounge and into the never-never.

Our groups' collective energy continued to thrive as we experimented with pendulums – watching on in amazement as the little beads on the end of our cotton threads spun and danced, yet our hands holding the cotton thread remained completely still. We ate nourishing home-cooked food that soothed our souls, we took long leisurely strolls through the picturesque bushland surrounding our cottage, as we contemplated life and exchanged stories, and then, there was the Reiki.

Florence, as a trained Reiki Master-Teacher, attuned each of us to Reiki. An attunement is a spiritual ceremony performed to connect a person to Reiki; the energy of the Universe. After our attunement ceremonies, we all exchanged stories. Some people saw other spirits moving amongst us, while others saw magnificent colours and felt all sorts of wonderful tingles and sensations as the Reiki energy began coursing through their bodies. I however, felt nothing and I didn't see much either.

I didn't feel any different after my attunement and I was so disappointed. Those old, all-too-familiar habitual thoughts began creeping back into my naïve and fragile mind: *You're not good enough. You're not as special as the others.* I thought there must have been something wrong with me because I wasn't having a mind-blowing experience like everyone else there that day. But I persisted with the training and Florie assured me that even though I wasn't feeling anything, it was still working just fine.

I soldiered on like a good student. My innate desire to please all teachers who have crossed my path is a force that has driven me to try and excel my entire life, and this instance was no exception. I trusted Florie, and I absolutely believed in her. How could I possibly deny what I had witnessed – all those amazing stories from the others? And my incredible experience that day in the living room was not to be ignored. So I knuckled down and kept going. I was going to heal myself.

4

HEAL, LOVE, LEARN

'I was home.'

It took me weeks of experimenting with healings and countless phone calls to Florie, as I practised the Reiki techniques on myself. Gradually, I began to physically feel something moving through my body; a subtle sensation of little ripples deep inside me. My hands began to tingle, albeit ever so slightly. And the more I practised, the stronger the tingles became. It felt like an electric current moving through my hands but it wasn't painful or even uncomfortable. It just felt different.

Soon, the colours started appearing before my closed eyes – all the colours of the rainbow and more. The colours morphed into abstract silhouettes; animals, constellations, people. I was performing healings on myself while I watched with great interest the kaleidoscope of colours and seemingly random shapes that kept appearing in front of me.

I was hooked. I wanted more! I returned to Florence two months later to do my Reiki level two attunement. This time, it was at her home and we were a very small group of five. It was a day-long workshop and it was packed full of training and life lessons. It was here that I experienced another vision. Remember the vision of the little yellow car rolling over? This time, however, I knew exactly what was happening and why so I was no longer afraid. In fact, I was beside myself with excitement!

One of the ladies in our group sat next to me during a break in our training and offered to help me work on my own gift. She sensed there was still something within me that hadn't been unleashed, and she knew I was ready.

We sat together as a group, as she explained that she was going to open herself up so I could access her soul. She was opening the virtual door to her own soul energy to let me in. I knew this was getting deep! I had by this stage, learned the basics about soul energy and universal energy and I knew that all the colours and shapes I had been seeing were forms of energy moving in and around me. But to have the ability to access someone else's energy and catch a glimpse into their life – into their past? I closed my eyes. Boy, was I nervous. But I was pumped. Bring it on.

There was a room flooded with natural light. As the vision became clearer, I could make out small details in the room. I saw native Australian wildflowers in a vase, intricate details on the floor mat, and an old-fashioned timber window frame. I saw sunlight beaming into the room and highlighting the dust particles as they danced their spontaneous dance in mid-air. I went outside to the back porch overlooking the property. I could see gum trees in the distance, and just beyond the back porch lay a tubby little pond with goldfish gliding through its green, algae-laden water.

No one else said a word. I opened my eyes to see the others watching me with admiring smiles on their faces. My eyes met this incredible lady's gaze.

'That, dear Jo, was my property in New South Wales,' she whispered. 'I lived there for many years and it holds a special place in my heart.'

I had perfectly described her rural oasis on the mainland; the room was where she worked most days and the porch overlooking the pond and the rest of the property was one of her favourite places to be, to relax and unwind. It was remarkable that I had never in my life heard of or visited this place myself. I had only met this lady just a few short hours ago and knew nothing about her or her private life, yet I was able to see all this through my vision.

That vision of mine will forever stay with me, nestled inside the folds of my heart to be cherished forever. The kindness shown to me that day was inspirational. She didn't have to help me, yet she did it anyway out of the kindness of her heart and now, many years later, I am trying hard to keep that kindness-momentum going. My spiritual awakening, as I like to call it, from that day on was officially full steam ahead.

My healings on myself were ticking along nicely. I was feeling and looking healthier and happier every day. The healing was happening from the inside out; as the universal energy healed and soothed my soul energy, my body and eventually my mind were also responding. Different images would come into focus, as I lay on my bed with my eyes closed, my hands gently resting on my body as the energy pulsed through me.

One of the more predominant and frequently appearing images was an odd-shaped star. Whenever this star of mine made an appearance during my healings, it became so familiar and comforting to me that it made me smile. It made me feel like I was home. Like there was no place I needed to be except right there, in my own private inner-sanctum, watching my pulsating odd-shaped, stunning star put on another show for me. I could have been anywhere on the planet and not felt one little bit home-sick or lost.

This realisation of *home* being inside me, and not at some geographical location was a critical turning point of my healing journey. I was home. *I am home.*

I had a consistent routine happening where I was dedicating an hour of every other day to doing a healing on myself. This sacred hour of mine was usually of an evening, either just after dinner or just before bedtime. Every single time, I would get out my Reiki training notes and a pen and paper for notetaking and retreat to my bedroom. I couldn't do my healings with music in my ears back then – it was too distracting. I needed sweet silence.

My family respected my new ritual, although they didn't understand it. Despite this time in my life being one of the most significant, I felt terribly lonely. I wanted desperately to tell all my family and friends what was happening to me, but I was afraid. Would they judge me? Call me crazy? Tell me it's not real and that it's all in my head? The thought of being criticized by my family and friends worried me, so I stayed silent. My only solace was my journal.

For a year, I eagerly scribbled down all my experiences in my journal. For a year, I barely told any other soul what was happening to me. My husband was tolerant and kind, but he soon grew tired of my constant ramblings about energy and spirits and visions and healings, bless his heart, so I stopped talking to him about it.

I turned to my aunty, my mother's sister, who welcomed my stories and eventually my healings with open arms. She was the one person who I felt was truly interested in what I was going through. But still, I felt lonely.

I felt like I was slowly drifting away from my close friends and this was for no other reason than I was changing, and fast. I was craving time with people who had already been through or were currently going through the same thing as me. I needed to connect with like-minded people, so I could feel like I wasn't a weirdo nutcase.

I joined a local meditation group. I reunited myself with regular yoga classes, for I had previously let these go when life got busy.

For me, an introvert, this was not an easy task; going out and meeting new groups of people, hoping I would fit in.

One thing I have constantly wrestled with for as long as I can remember, is the desire to fit in. I wanted to be the kind of person that everyone would love, and if I ever thought I had upset someone – even inadvertently – it would crush me. I wanted to be popular at school, I wanted the cool kids to like me and in the process, I didn't appreciate the circle of friends I already had. I pretended to be someone else, hoping they would accept me.

This need to belong has been weighing me down my entire life, and although I was loving every second of my spiritual journey, I was still embarrassed and possibly even ashamed of it. So I kept it hidden. I kept my true self, who was just coming into her own, hidden. The only time I allowed myself to stop the self-judgement and criticism and doubt was during my hour-long healing sessions. It was only during those hourly sessions that all else was left behind; all thoughts, doubts, fears, expectations, frustrations.

I looked forward to my healing hour as if it were time spent with an old, dear friend. I could be me! The *real* me, not some fake representation of who I thought I should be. It was a relief to let go, even if only for that one hour. Amazingly, despite my attempts to hide my new passion, the healings were working their magic on me and my physical health was dramatically improving. It would take many more years of self-love and regular healings for my mind to get a grip, to enable my mental health to heal.

As I slowly started to trust that I could tell other people what I was doing in regard to healings, I began practising my craft on willing family and friends, and they too were starting to see the benefits. It came as a shock to me that there were, in fact, some people in my life who were open to the concept of energy healing. I continued to keep my developing psychic visions and spirit encounters under wraps because that would be taking things too far — for me to expect people to believe that I could now hear the whisperings of ghosts.

As I continued to perform healings on myself and those first, select few family and friends, I began to develop the ability to hear messages and conversations from the spirit realm. Not only that, I was developing the ability to see inside a person's body, along with the ability to feel their aches and pains and other physical sensations inside my own body.

The thought of admitting any of this to my peers would send images through my head of them in fits, rolling around on the floor, laughing until the tears rolled down their faces and their sides were aching from the effort. Or I imagined them gaping at me in disbelief, as if I had just done a triple somersault from a standing position on solid ground and landed it to perfection. Yeh, nah. I wasn't ready for that type of humiliation. Good old self-doubt was still sneakily playing its hand, keeping my true potential just at bay for a little while longer.

Putting all my irrational thoughts aside, there was no doubt my healings were now helping other people. My dear mum was noticing significant improvements in her chronic neck and shoulder pain she had been suffering with for years and years. After receiving a few Reiki treatments from me, she confessed one day.

'I don't know what you're doing to me or how you're doing it, so it's a little bit creepy, but something is happening to me that I can't explain,' she said. 'I feel so happy now! And it's not just relief from the pain, it's more than that. I feel different. I feel great!'

Now let me just explain a little something about my mum: she had a Catholic upbringing, and she is your typical sceptic of all things supernatural. And she doesn't mind saying so either. So *my mum* singing the praises of energy healing had me feeling very chuffed with myself. I had cautiously poked a foot out of my spiritual closet and although it was – much to my amusement – creeping her out, she was embracing my proverbial foot with open arms.

What would I have done, had she not embraced my beliefs and this new version of me? Honestly, I am not sure. Perhaps I may have tucked it all back in the closet and kept it that way – for a few more years, at least.

What would my sternly-sensible and logically-thinking, seriously-devout-to-Western-Medicine, frustratingly-anti-Eastern-Medicine-and-anything-even-remotely-alternative father have said, had he still been alive during the unveiling of my spiritual awakening? Dad's passing, around eighteen months before I embarked on my first Reiki Retreat, was one of the toughest things I have lived through. Dad had struggled with type one diabetes and with the toll it took on his body almost his entire adult life. And in his later years, cancer reared its ugly head.

His illness took its toll on our whole family, as we watched him slowly and painfully waste away. His body had finally had enough of the struggle.

Mum, my sister and I all sat by his bedside, holding his hand. We couldn't bear to watch him suffer another second.

'It's okay to go dad, it's time to say goodbye,' whispered my sister and I.

He held on as long as he could. He was so afraid. He made us promise to take care of mum. He made us promise that his grandkids would never forget him. Then, peacefully and silently, he was gone. In September of 2013, in his sixty-fifth year of this lifetime on Earth, dad's soul crossed over from this reality and into the spirit realm.

When we lose someone we love, it takes a part of us away forever. We are forever changed. The sense of loss when a loved one dies is numbing.

As a family, together, united by our sorrow, we grieved dad's loss. And as his daughter, in my own private time, I grieved the loss of my only, far-from-perfect-but-I-loved-him-anyway father – mostly in the wee hours of the mornings when the canopy of the dark night held me safely in its embrace. I would sob and my husband would hold me tight, there in the darkness, and he would not let me go until long after I had cried myself to sleep.

Dad's death has undoubtedly played a part in my spiritual awakening. His spirit was there at that first Reiki Retreat. Florie told me she could feel him, but he was keeping his distance. He was lingering in the gigantic pine trees that lined the entrance to the property; she said he didn't want to interfere with my experience and that he wanted to observe from afar.

Did I believe her? I truly wanted to! It was a lovely story and it comforted me. My scepticism at the time may have prevented me from truly appreciating that encounter with dad's soul that day, but that's okay. I truly appreciate it now. So would dad have welcomed the spiritualist me without reservation or judgement, had he still been walking this Earth? Probably not. And yes, that probably would have put the brakes on my spiritual growth for a while.

But I believe everything happens for a reason. I believe there are no coincidences. Everything plays out just as it is meant to, at exactly the time it is meant to. Sometimes, through the choices we make, our willpower or our ego or our intellect may cause some ripples in the grand plan that I believe is mapped out for us all. Our free-will comes into play often, but this intricate and ever-knowing, ever-present universal energy that we are all a part of steers us in the general direction that we are all destined to be travelling, as individuals and as a collective.

Before too long my little business was born. I always knew what my healing business would be called; I would name it after my super-awesome star that was still loyally visiting me during my healing sessions. I named my business *Reiki Star*. I bought myself a massage table, created a business profile on social media, and began sharing my stories with my community.

Within a few days, a lady saw my profile and contacted me for a healing. And then another. And another. They all loved the healings so much, they were sending their mothers, fathers, sisters, best friends, work colleagues, aunties and uncles, cousins and neighbours to me.

And so the word-of-mouth cycle went on, and now my little healing business is flourishing. I now incorporate Reiki with my own intuitive healing techniques to offer my clients an eclectic and unique healing experience. My gift has evolved at high speed since I first started. I currently offer services including private healing sessions, group classes, Reiki training and spiritual mentoring.

I may not be a famous healer with thirty, or twenty, or even ten years experience behind me. But I am a real person, facing the everyday challenges of raising a young family, keeping my marriage fresh and interesting, paying bills, maintaining friendships that are important to me, growing my business, prioritising *me* time, developing my spiritual gifts, making mistakes, working through illnesses, loving deeply and openly, and helping others as often as I can.

I'm not draped in mystery. I'm not an unapproachable, unrelatable icon on a pedestal. I'm an everyday mum, wife, daughter, sister, and friend, who just happens to have a very deep connection to Spirit and who has lived through some powerful life lessons.

I am now sharing all the lessons and skills I have learned in the past few years, particularly those learned since my spiritual awakening. This stuff isn't for me; it's for *all of us*. People can see

I have a genuine desire to help them, and they are coming to me for healings and guidance and training in droves. I am now doing what I love as a means of providing for my family, and for this, I am eternally grateful. I truly couldn't ask for a more rewarding or humbling job.

Every day, I see people who were previously either depressed, anxious, chronically ill, fatigued, emotional, stressed or lost, come bounding into my treatment room a few short days or weeks later, oozing happiness. And the *joy* this brings me is almost impossible to articulate. Sometimes, all it takes is one healing or mentoring session. Other times, it takes a few more.

I believe the evidence to support energy healing, and to living a life that is more than just one-dimensional is crystal clear. I've lived it myself, and I've witnessed it in countless others. The consistent, overwhelmingly positive feedback I receive from clients and readers near and far makes my heart sing:

'Thank you so much for bringing our little man home to us. He is so much more present and far chattier. Most of all, thanks for starting the healing process between him and I… massive, massive turn around!' – From a mother who sought my services, because she felt disconnected from her toddler son.

'With her easy going and heart-felt approach, Jo has given me the boost to believe deeper in my abilities. To understand and feel energy and to accept the healing light we all deserve. Within one session I felt a weight lift from me in golden waves which created a deep sense of peace upon release.' – From a lady who sought my services, wanting to explore her true potential on a deeper level.

'Jo has been helping me peel away the layers to my issues. Bit

by bit, I am feeling the difference to my personal space. I have been searching for answers for over twenty years and have finally come to the right person to get things sorted!' – From an older gentleman who sought my services, because he felt terribly unhappy and lonely.

'I felt so foggy and lethargic today and struggled to get out of bed. I missed the start [of the online healing] as I was reading in the sun and suddenly felt a huge influx of energy and clarity. I jumped on for the last bit of your group healing. Thank you so much. Feeling like a different person!' – From a lady who was having a rough start to her day. She felt the energy from one of my online healings, before she even knew it was under way.

I am now able to reach more people through an online community of readers who actively participate in healings that I broadcast live through social media, and the numbers are increasing by the day. I am teaching others how to heal themselves and their loved ones by harnessing energy, through Reiki and other means. I am running guided meditation classes; taking myself to that energetic realm somewhere between our reality and the next, where I connect with Spirit. I then take the class on their own unique channelled meditation journey, custom-made by their Spirit Guides and Higher Beings.

My gift is constantly evolving and expanding, and it's happening fast. Clear communication with other souls, living and deceased, is now a normal part of my day. These messages provide clarity, comfort and guidance and you will find a selection of these messages in *Part IV* of this book.

I use the energy of the Universe, through Reiki and my own intuitive healing techniques, to help and heal. I experience psychic visions which add extra elements of depth and understanding to the healing and spiritual growth process. And I have an unwavering inner knowing that everyone is capable of all the above, to varying degrees, and so much more. *Everyone, including you.* You can do it, if you want to. Let this book guide you through the wondrous world of spirituality and energy, so you too can discover the extraordinary.

My wish is that this book, at the very least, will encourage you to go and live your life exactly the way you want to. Be brave. Be fierce. Be kind. Love hard. Find your inner goddess / god. Go and be your own organic, authentic self and then shine your light for others, so they are encouraged to shine their beautiful light, too. x

PART II

THE NITTY GRITTY

So that's me. That is my story, so far.

And there are more stories from me, and from other people, woven amongst the rest of this book because I find the best way for me to teach and for you to learn, is through examples and storytelling. We should all tell more stories. Tell your kids your stories – good and bad. Listen when your parents and grandparents share their stories with you. Everyone has a story and within each story is magic and mystery, drama and suspense, love and happiness. Every story is a journey.

Let me now share with you everything I have learned on my journey. My mind is brimming with information that I can't share in the space of a few short minutes either side of a healing, or even during a several-hour workshop. There is simply too much. This information, to me, is gold and I hope you think so too. It makes sense. And it needs to be shared.

I know that everything I have learned on my spiritual journey was not solely for my own benefit. I knew that from day one. Years ago, I knew I would someday be writing this book. And here it is.

5

SPIRITUAL ENERGY: WHAT IS IT, REALLY?

'The lessons and the experiences never grow old; it will never bore you.'

Soul energy. Universal energy. Earth energy. Energetic frequencies. Chakras. Light.

Having a basic understanding of spiritual energy in its various forms creates the foundation for developing your intuition, for connecting and communicating with the energies in and around you, for healing your mind, body and soul, for finding true love (of self and of others), and for discovering your soul purpose. And this is all just the tip of the iceberg.

Spiritual energy is an intelligent, all-knowing force that works in very mysterious ways. And I don't believe that we, in our human form, will ever know the full capabilities, potential or reach of spiritual energy. But this is not as bad as it sounds. In fact because of this, spiritual energy is perhaps the greatest teacher of all. Whether you have just learned the basics, or whether you have been researching spiritual energy for half a lifetime, you will always be learning something new and discovering or witnessing something you never thought possible. This is so exciting! The lessons and the experiences never grow old; it will never bore you.

The wondrous world of spiritual energy is accessible to everyone, including you, and as you read on you will realise it doesn't need to be an overwhelming topic that can't be grasped. Please read on to learn more about the different types of energy and my interpretation of them all.

SOUL ENERGY

There is a mostly unseen and often misunderstood life force that radiates within every single one of us. It is what makes us breathe, walk, talk, function. It drives us. It is our soul energy. Literally, our life force.

We all know of and have a general understanding of electricity. Electricity is the energy that gives life to things like televisions, household appliances and light globes. We can't see it, but we know it's there; flowing through wires and sockets and providing power for those lucky enough to have it in their home or workplace. Soul or life energy is the same. It flows through us, and although most people can't see it with their naked eye, this energy is as real as it gets. Soul energy contributes to an inanimate mass of flesh, muscles and bones becoming a living, breathing human being.

Have you ever heard the expression: *Someone just walked over my grave?* This sensation that most of us have experienced – that intense shiver that shoots through the body without warning – is your soul energy responding to or communicating with another energy around you. Once you acknowledge you have soul energy coursing through your body, you will likely become aware of other subtle little sensations that usually can't be explained by science or Western Medicine.

You can achieve immeasurable amounts of happiness and success when you are connecting and communicating with your soul energy. To do this, you need to develop and strengthen your intuition or your gut instincts. You may also develop a strong inner knowing about things which at times, may totally baffle you because you may not fully understand it, but you must learn to trust it.

For example, you're driving to work along the same route you travel each day, when suddenly you feel the need to take a detour, although you have no idea why. You listen to that inner knowing, drive the alternative route, and you arrive at work on time.

Your colleague, who takes the same route to work that you usually do, arrived at work an hour late because of the unscheduled major roadworks that held up traffic. That unexplainable *need* you felt, to divert your course of travel, is your soul energy sending you a message. So when those feelings or thoughts pop in, learn to pay attention because the more you acknowledge and then act on those feelings, the stronger your intuition will become.

When you have a strong connection to your soul energy, you will learn to speak and act from your heart with conviction. Your soul energy, is you! It is the real you, beneath the layers of behaviours and habits created to protect yourself from being hurt or manipulated or humiliated; beneath those conceptual masks that we all wear from time to time.

Soul energy doesn't only exist in human bodies. Soul energy also exists in the space, or the universal energy, around us all. These types of soul energies are commonly referred to as spirits, ghosts, higher beings or guardian angels. I have learned that these types of soul energies are not to be feared; they are to be respected, just like we would respect another human. From my own communication with Spirit, I have learned that we humans have all been allocated Guardian Angels or Spirit Guides who will stay close by, watch over us, protect us and provide us with guidance when we need it.

Acknowledging your own guides regardless of whether you can see, sense or feel them right now, is the first step in establishing a beautifully powerful and rewarding relationship with these otherworldly beings who want nothing more than to help and guide you. I began talking to my guides long before I could hear them responding. And yes, I felt a little silly at the time, talking to someone or something that I wasn't sure even existed, but it was a great challenge for me to learn to trust what I couldn't yet see or feel.

I now hear my guides communicating with me through visions and through thoughts in my head that aren't mine. Not only that, I now communicate with the vast array of other Spirit Beings who are out there in the spiritual realm, helping and teaching us humans.

I would now like to discuss dark spirits and negative entities because I think it's important we all have a better understanding of these often-misunderstood entities. Some spiritualists and healers will tell you there is no such thing, however I have had encounters with a handful of dark spirits and I want to give you my current perception of them, in the hope that you will no longer fear them like many people do. Most of the time, these negative entities are what I call *lost*.

Their energy has become low and imbalanced. Often, they were released from their human body quickly by means of, say, a sudden and traumatic accident, which has resulted in their soul being stuck in between realms, and sometimes stuck in that exact location where they died. Their energy may become agitated, and the space around them may energetically become congested and heavy.

This is often why a place will become *haunted,* because the soul is stuck and simply can't find a way to move on to where it needs to go. I have helped many souls who were considered ghosts haunting a residence or building, cross over. Most of them don't mean to cause any harm or scare anyone. Yes, some of them have a very dark energy about them, but I am not afraid of them because my energy is high and strong and powerful and my Spirit Guides are protecting me, therefore I *know* they can't hurt me.

These dark spirits need *love* and *healing*. I can't stress this enough — everyone, even spirits, needs love. Their energy needs a chance to be renewed and recharged; to be revitalised.

Imagine if a human was trapped in a place they couldn't escape — would you want to help them? Would you feel compassion for that human? Spirits are the same as us, they just don't have a physical body to reside in. I find this comparison helps many people learn to respect spirits and no longer fear them. I think a lot of this fear comes from not being able to see, feel or touch them. This *uncertainty* is likely the cause of the fear, so if we remove some of the stigma around spirits by learning more about them and by thinking of them as an energy form, there will be less fear.

Soul energy, like all spiritual energy, is about as complex as it gets but we can still learn to connect with it, work with it, heal it, be one with it. Perhaps you are now inspired to dive deep into the how, what, when, or why of soul energy, or perhaps you are now satisfied with this basic introduction. If you are going to explore it further, do so with as much humility and love as you can muster, and your explorations will serve you well.

Throughout all my encounters with soul energy in all its various expressions, I have learned one thing: to always respect it and to never have any expectations. Many of my experiences with soul energy cannot be expressed in words and some of the things I have seen have confused my poor, human brain with their mysticism and other-worldly-ness! My brain now knows not to over-analyse or over-think these encounters, and I believe this act of surrendering to the experience is opening me up to witnessing more and more each day. I now just smile, and thank my lucky stars that I can witness glimpses of the magic that is soul energy.

It is common for children to see or sense other souls around them. Has your child ever had a conversation with someone who wasn't there? Has your child ever told you there is something in her bedroom? Your child is tuning into the energies around her, and this is nothing to be afraid of. Here are some tips for how you can help your child: Instead of calling them Ghosts, call them Guardian Angels.

The word 'ghost' doesn't have a good reputation and can often instil fear. Everyone loves angels! Angels connotate images of beautiful beings who are always happy and kind. Through making this simple reference switch, your child (and you!) will learn to embrace, not fear, the souls around her. Mostly, the souls close to children are grandparents or great-grandparents who have passed and who are now with their family in spirit.

If your child is experiencing any of this, or more, there are other tips throughout this book suggesting ways you can help your child navigate the wondrous world of energy. Refer to 'children' in the Index at the back of the book, to easily access this information.

I am so very excited for you to be learning about soul energy, because having this knowledge can change your perception of everything and everyone including, most importantly, yourself.

AURAS

Our soul energy has external layers that extend from our soul energy and radiate outwards. These layers are called auras. They often appear to those who can see them, as colourful layers surrounding a person. To others, they appear as a haziness or a distortion of the air around a person – much like the heat waves that shimmy off a tarred and sealed road on a hot day.

A surprisingly high number of children of all ages can see other peoples' auras, however they don't often mention it to others because to them, it is an entirely normal occurrence they have witnessed their entire lives. How wonderful that it doesn't occur to children to mind! So if your child ever tells you he can see colours around people, don't be alarmed! This is an incredible gift your child has, and you can help him to embrace this gift simply by having open conversations about the colours he sees.

Your aura can protect you, and it can help you to help others. You can learn to strengthen your aura, when you feel threatened or vulnerable. You can learn to extend or stretch out your aura, when you feel someone around you needs some extra love and support. In the self-care section of this book you will learn ways to do this, and more.

I did a healing recently for a woman who was prone to absorbing other people's negative energy. We determined this was mostly due to her auric layers not functioning properly. As the healing progressed, my entire body was reacting to her auric layers being activated and strengthened. Her aura was healing fast and as the layers healed, they began to pulse and throb: moving slowly but very firmly outwards, pushing not just my hands, but my entire body backwards and away from the woman on the table. Her auric layers then retracted, drawing my entire body towards her like a big magnet.

I found myself pacing backwards a few steps, and then forwards a few steps, over and over, in sync with her fluctuating aura, as it regained strength and began flexing its energetic muscles. It was a surreal experience!

The layers of your aura are interconnected with your soul energy and with your body, and they serve many different functions. They are also a good indication of how healthy, happy and connected to Spirit you are.

There are many healers who work closely with the auric layers of a person, and they can identify imbalances that need healing, and even provide spiritual guidance based on how they interpret or read the aura. Although this is not an area I specialise in, I will from time to time do auric healings for a person, if that is where my attention is drawn; much like the healing of the lady with the malfunctioning auras.

Your aura is an elaborate energy form, designed to add depth to your soul energy. Your aura not only enhances your spiritual intelligence, it is also intended to enhance your entire human experience.

CHAKRAS

Chakra is a Sanskrit word meaning wheel or disc. Chakras are energy wheels located at different points of the body, and if they aren't spinning or moving freely or they have become blocked or out of sync with one another for whatever reason, they can mess with your overall health and happiness.

Making sure that your chakras are spinning correctly is an important part of your healing journey, and there are many healers who offer chakra balancing as a service. When I am doing a healing for a client, I hold my hands above their body, over each of their chakras, and I can feel the energy there. I can determine whether the chakra is balanced and spinning freely or whether it needs some tender loving care.

There are seven major chakras in the human body, generally represented by different colours and symbols, and each of these chakras are intricately connected to various other parts of the body and soul energy. There are many ways you can balance your own chakras, including meditation and crystal healing.

On the following page is a basic introduction to the seven major chakras, and their spiritual and energetic functions. Keep in mind, these are the most common traits of the chakras, and not necessarily the only traits.

THE SEVEN MAJOR CHAKRAS

Root Chakra

Location: Base of spine

Colour: Red

Function: Grounding, safety

Sacral Chakra

Location: Just below the navel (lower abdomen)

Colour: Orange

Function: Emotions, creativity, sexuality

Solar Plexus Chakra

Location: Stomach (upper abdomen)

Colour: Yellow

Function: Personal power, identity, intellect

Heart Chakra

Location: Centre of chest

Colour: Green

Function: Compassion, love

Throat Chakra

Location: Throat

Colour: Blue

Function: Personal truth, expression

Third Eye Chakra

Location: Between the eyes

Colour: Indigo

Function: Intuition, inspiration

Crown Chakra

Location: Top of head

Colour: Violet

Function: Wisdom, transcendence

⋘ ⋙

As with all other energy, chakras cannot be seen with the naked eye by most people. They are perfect little spinning wheels of energy, working together to keep our soul energy and our body balanced.

EARTH ENERGY

Let's talk about Earth energy for a moment. If soul energy drives us, then Earth energy drives our beautiful planet. Earth energy is the life source of our planet. Those delicious tingles you feel in your hand when you hold your favourite crystal or the subtle buzz you feel in your bare feet when you stand on wet grass is Earth energy.

Everything from Mother Nature has her energy flowing through it. Rocks, trees, grass, soil, sand, water, flowers, and of course crystals and gemstones all have Earth energy flowing through them. They are all alive, in their own unique and beautiful way.

When you go to the beach and your bare feet nestle in the sand, does it make you feel positively radiant? When you venture into the bush for a hike, or a leisurely stroll through nature, does it make you feel re-energized? Connecting with the energy from our delicately powerful planet recharges our soul energy.

The importance of Earth energy – of Mother Nature – is often underestimated and a lot of the time, the sheer power of Earth energy goes unnoticed. If you can acknowledge that all of nature carries with it an energetic force that is incredibly healing, and then give yourself opportunities to connect with this energy, you will almost immediately notice the positive impact it has on you.

Learning to connect with and work with Earth energy will not only benefit you, it will also benefit our beautiful planet. When we connect with another energy, there is an exchange. So in this instance, you receive energy from Earth to strengthen and heal, and Earth receives your energy – your love – giving the Earth more strength and vitality.

Mother Earth is also capable of renewing expired or negative energy – she is like a gigantic recycling facility, transforming the old into new. There are many ways in which you can work with Earth energy, but probably the most popular techniques are the act of earthing or grounding, and working with crystals and gemstones, all of which will be discussed in more detail later in this chapter.

UNIVERSAL ENERGY

Universal energy is the mothership of energies! Universal energy is everywhere – it is inside us and is all around us, our little planet, other planets and galaxies, and beyond. It is an infinite blanket of energy. The Universe, to me, is what others consider to be God. The Universe is an ever-present ever-knowing complex and perfectly crafted entity of energetic love and light.

Whilst some people of faith pray to their God, I pray to the Universe. Let me just take a moment of pause here, to clarify that I do not identify as being a religious person. Nor am I a person who disapproves of religious circles or other beliefs and practices.

My well-intentioned non-practicing Catholic mum tried to introduce me to religion when I was six years old. She dropped me off at Sunday School – a weekend bible study group for children – and then she came home, planning to get some chores done while she had the house to herself. I walked through the back door ten minutes later.

I had walked home, by myself, after realising in a few short minutes I was not compatible with what was being taught in that little room of our local church. Mum quickly learned that religion, in that context, wasn't a good fit for me. That was the first and last time I went to Sunday School.

As an adult, I have learned that I am a believer in the Divine – in a greater force that we, in our human forms, will likely never come close to fully understanding or comprehending.

I appreciate and respect that everyone on this planet has different beliefs. I now prefer to hand-pick little bits and pieces from each religion, each belief, each personal opinion of others, each spiritual practice, for my ever-growing and ever-changing basket of personal growth and joy.

I enjoy some aspects of Buddhism, some of Christianity, some of the other varied religions, some of the supernatural, some of witchcraft and paganism. I am tenderly and lovingly plucking those morsels which tantalise my personal tastebuds from the smorgasbord of beliefs and practices and I respectfully acknowledge and let go of the rest.

Universal energy is everything and everyone, as one. It is an intelligent entity born from the collective intertwining of all other energies and frequencies; all life, love, thoughts, memories, matter, planets, atmospheres, galaxies, realms. So when I speak of the Universe, it is this context I am referring to.

The Universe would easily be the most elaborate of all spiritual energies, in my opinion. It baffles me and excites me all at once.

When I experience glimpses of what Universal energy is doing – how it is interacting with other energies, and the effect it is having on them – sometimes all I can do in response is shake my head in shock and admiration. I certainly don't understand it in its entirety, but the messages I have received from Spirit and the visions I have witnessed are enough to assure me that we are all very much in this together and because we are all one with the Universe – because we all *are* the Universe – we are all capable of so much more than we could perhaps ever realise – more love, more opportunities, deeper relationships, more joy, better health, and so much more.

If you can acknowledge this Universal entity that lives in and around you, and you then learn to connect and communicate with it, you'd better prepare yourself for a whole lot of *magic* to unfold.

Spirits, angels and higher beings are all around us – guiding us, teaching us, healing and nurturing us. The energy of the Universe strengthens us and unites us. The Earth's energy grounds us and connects us. All these infinite energies are so delicately intertwined with one another, creating an intricate energetic ecosystem.

6

THE SYNERGY OF SPIRITUAL ENERGY

'We are filled with love and light and
we are surrounded by love and light.'

All forms of spiritual energy have a synergistic relationship with one another. And not only this, they all have the capacity to change. They can *meld* together, they can *evolve*, they can *upgrade*, they can *communicate*, and they can *teach*. They can all interact with each other and depending on how strong your relationship is with spiritual energy, you too may catch glimpses of all this, and more. The synergy of spiritual energy is constant, and although there may be fluctuations and changes to this synergy, it is ever-lasting.

Spiritual energy is like water. Imagine taking a delicate little teacup and filling it with water. Then imagine pouring this cup of water into an ocean. That tiny cup of water suddenly becomes one with the vast ocean; ebbing and flowing with the tide, as it is moved by the gravitational force of the moon and the sun. That tiny cup of water is dispersed in, and becomes intertwined with, that entire ocean.

When energies combine, they too become one. They blend and merge and flow, just like that little teacup of water. How does energy do this? I believe that while we are here in this human form, we will never fully understand spiritual energy. It is far too complex and vast for us to fully comprehend. But through working with energy and communicating with energy all the time, every day, I am learning as I go.

Some of the experiences I have had blow my mind and they constantly test my boundaries of what I think I already know about energy. Sometimes the various energies will show me, through visions, of how they are interacting with each other. And sometimes I will simply feel the energy.

I can feel how it is moving and flowing in and around a person. It is through these varied interactions with energy that I have learned to keep a very open mind, and to expect the unexpected and this is something that excites me so much!

Communicating with energy is one of the most rewarding things I have had the pleasure of experiencing. I am certain that the glimpses I am shown, of how various spiritual energies interact and what they are all capable of, is a drop in the ocean of what is really happening. This keeps me humble and keeps me hungry to learn and experience more.

I don't expect to fully understand energy in this lifetime, but it has taught me so much and continues to teach me every day.

COMMUNICATION OF SPIRITUAL ENERGY

One way of communicating or transmitting spiritual energy is through brain waves and sound waves. Therefore your thoughts, your intention and your spoken words are all ways to transfer or communicate energy. Brain waves and sound can both be observed and recorded using modern technology, so for most people there is no doubt these invisible transmissions are real. Even though we can't see them, they still exist.

Try thinking of these invisible transmissions from an energetic perspective, and you will then realise the effect these transmissions are having on your own and other people's soul energy. Not only this, think of what type of energy these invisible transmissions are sending out to the Universe.

If you are having positive thoughts, words or emotions, you are projecting positive energy onto whoever or whatever is at the receiving end. This can have an incredible impact on the receiver. The phrase *'sending you lots of love'* may sound familiar to you. This is a phrase often used when someone is having a bad day, or has just experienced a loss, and you want to cheer them up or let them know they are in your thoughts.

These words, whether spoken, written on a card or simply held in your thoughts, are transmitting a whole lot of positive and loving spiritual energy to the receiver. You are essentially sending this person healing, through your energetic interaction with them.

Spiritual energy can also be communicated through the five senses: touch, taste, sight, smell and sound. Here's an example: if someone is psychic, it doesn't just mean they can hear Spirit talking to them. The communication may be through any of the five senses or can be an inner knowing or can even be through dreams. Some people can communicate through one of these means, whereas other people can communicate through several or all of these means.

Perhaps, as you read through this book and work through the exercises and healings, you too may begin to develop the ability to communicate with other energies around you, including the soul energy of people living and passed. Although this is not the main intention or focus of this book, if this is something you are hoping to achieve, then reading this book and embracing the activities may very well open you up to spirit communication.

Should this happen to you, if it feels good and right then there's no reason why you can't explore this new gift you are developing. If it feels uncomfortable and even frightens you a little, then please know you have the ability to control whatever it is that is happening to you.

Opening yourself up to spiritual energy can result in incredible experiences and it can transform your whole world, but you need to trust it. If things start happening to you that you aren't ready for, use the power of your thoughts to either slow things down or stop it completely. Or seek the help of a healer you trust. Then one day, when you feel you are ready, you can try again.

I need to emphasize here: energy is nothing to be afraid of.

Some experiences may leave you feeling unsettled or vulnerable, but if you can follow my lead throughout this book, trust your intuition and have fun along the way, you will come to love energy, and communicating with energy, as much as I do! I also encourage you to recognise the true power of your thoughts and words, because these are a simple yet effective way to spread love far and wide. You will be communicating good vibes to yourself and to others, and to anything else you choose.

ENERGETIC FREQUENCIES

Think of a radio – how it can tune to different channels or frequencies. Much like these radio frequencies, spiritual energy also has different frequencies or levels. If the spiritual frequency is low, the energy will become negative, weak and dim.

On the flip side, if the spiritual frequency is high, the energy will become positive, strong and clear. And much like a radio changes channels, spiritual energy can change frequencies too. This is an important part of the healing process; to raise your energetic frequency. The higher the frequency, the better you will feel and the happier you will be.

Your own, and other people's, negative thoughts, words, emotions, or trauma will impact on and potentially lower your frequency. And on the other hand positive thoughts, words, emotions and uplifting joyous experiences will raise your frequency.

It makes sense for us all to be working towards existing on as high a frequency as possible, so we can enjoy all the loveliness it has to offer. And of course, up there, we aren't as susceptible to the negative energy because we won't be on its frequency. Positive energy is drawn to other positive energy. And negative energy is drawn to other negative energy.

Negative energy will always be around you, in the form of other people's negative thoughts, words and emotions. But you won't be impacted by it as much if your energetic frequency is nice and high, because the contrasting frequencies aren't as compatible with each other.

Try to remember: like attracts like. Are you familiar with the *Law of Attraction*? It is a widely discussed theory that we are constantly attracting to us whatever we are putting out to the Universe. You get what you give. Keep your vibration as high as you can, and send out high vibe thoughts and words as often as you can, and you will attract more positivity and high-vibrational goodness into your life.

With this in mind, there are actions you can take immediately to raise your personal frequency and reap the rewards. If you are stuck for ideas, keep reading! There is a whole section in this book on things you can integrate into your everyday life which will help bring you greater happiness, better health, deeper connection to self, and a higher frequency! Hooray for good vibrations.

SPIRITUAL ENERGY AND DEATH

Does spiritual energy ever expire? No. If an energy ever becomes weak or compromised it either draws on other energy or it simply moves on, so it can meld with other energy, allowing it to strengthen or to change form or frequency. Energy is recycled. We are all soul energy residing in these vessels we call bodies. Death is the releasing of the soul from the body, thereby allowing the soul to continue its journey so it can fulfil its purpose.

A lady came to see me, courtesy of her adult children who thought she might benefit from an energy healing. Rosemary's daughter died three years ago and she still hadn't come to terms with her loss. Rose is a kind, older lady who is softly-spoken yet strong in constitution and she had never experienced energy healing. She knew nothing about it and had no idea what to expect.

Rose confided in me that the only way she had survived the past three years, was to shut out all memories of her daughter and of her daughter's death. She never spoke of her daughter after she passed; it was too painful. Rose felt as though her heart had closed and her emotions had vanished. She was functioning on autopilot.

Throughout the healing, Rosemary felt the energy of the Universe coursing through her body – despite this being her first time. The dialogue I shared with her – what I was feeling and experiencing – was a direct reflection of what she was feeling inside as the energy of loss, pain and anguish gently lifted from her soul. As we lightened this energetic load from her body, many of her chronic physical aches and pains completely vanished. No more aching shoulders, feet, chest or hips; her body is now pain-free.

Near the end of Rose's healing, I felt a very tangible love-energy surround her whole body. It gave me goose bumps from head to toe. I felt it envelope her – it cradled her with its love. This love-energy was filled with so much emotion – so much love for this woman laying on my table – it almost made me cry. But I didn't share this experience with Rose; I wasn't sure if she was ready for that. I did however, notice the tears that sprang from the corners of her eyes as it all silently unfolded.

When the healing ended, we were exchanging stories about what we both experienced and Rose – eyes filled with tears – told me she felt her daughter next to her. For the first time since her daughter's passing, she had allowed herself to be vulnerable and through this vulnerability, Rose was able to connect with her. Rose had opened her heart and soul and had let love back in.

Rosemary admitted to not believing in spirits prior to that day. She heard stories from others who felt her daughter's presence but she didn't believe them – it was simply their overactive imaginations.

Rose now *believes*, and this has made the burden of the loss she's been carrying for three years feel a little lighter. She is now feeling excited for her future and for the future of the rest of her family.

If you are grieving the loss of a loved one through death, take comfort in knowing death is not the end. Death is a small part of the soul journey. Your loved one is not far away, I promise you this.

I know this pales in comparison to having your loved one with you in the flesh, but it is a comfort. The need to physically touch a loved one and knowing that won't happen again in this lifetime, is excruciating. But to know they are right there with you in spirit, watching over you, communicating with you, sending you never ending love, is a very special knowledge indeed.

Death is a transition of energy – it is a form of energetic expansion and it is part of your – *of everyone's* – soul journey. Through death, we all move to the next chapter – not only for those who die but for those left behind here on Earth. I believe that death itself is not something to be feared or dreaded. I believe that death is a part of the circle of life (a little cliché I know, but hear me out) and without death, there can be no new life.

We are born, we live, we die. Some of our souls reincarnate –

to go through the cycle again – to learn more lessons and have more human experiences, while others remain in the spiritual realm.

Death brings new beginnings and it brings endings. The circle of life goes on. The *circle of energy* goes on.

Energy is pure love. Energy is light. Therefore, we are *all* pure love and light. We all have soul energy within us and these other powerful energetic forces around us; we are filled with love and light and we are surrounded by love and light. If we want to live a life of happiness and good health, we need to rediscover our own love and light. How do we do that? We heal!

We all have an ability to heal our bodies and our minds and our souls. In this book, you will learn just a few of the techniques millions of people throughout the world are using to heal themselves and achieve true happiness, myself included.

7

INTUITION

'Being intuitive instils confidence and
a deep sense of peace within.'

Often referred to as gut instinct, intuition is inner knowing. You know that feeling of dread that sits in the pit of your stomach when you know you're about to do something that you really shouldn't? That is your intuition trying to guide you. Fingers crossed, by the end of this chapter you will have a greater respect of your intuition and will be more inclined to listen when it is talking to you.

Your intuition is essentially your soul-self – your soul energy communicating with you. Your intuition can guide you through thick and thin, and if you choose to pay attention to what your intuition is telling you, your life will be transformed.

I would like to use this chapter to teach you some easy techniques that I use to help strengthen intuition and to help connect with intuition.

THE YES / NO TEST

This little test is about *feeling* your answer.

It's about disconnecting from your head for a moment and connecting with your heart and your soul energy. I would like to teach you how to feel a *yes* and a *no* response inside your body. This was the very first intuition technique I was ever taught, and although it took me a while to master, it has served me well over the years.

It has helped me with my own questions, and with those of my clients. Now I have to say, this technique isn't the easiest to learn – some people pick it up straight away, while others need to practise repeatedly before they get the hang of it. So please don't feel disheartened if you don't get this on the first or second or even the third go.

You need to be in a very relaxed state before attempting this for the first time. Perhaps, do the breathing meditation exercise on page 139 prior to attempting this technique, as it will help you relax. It is also a good idea to have someone help you for the first few attempts at this, so you can focus on nothing but relaxing and breathing.

Ask your helper to prepare a couple of questions to ask you. The questions need to be directed at you and need to have *yes* or *no* answers. They also need to be really obvious.

For example, *are you sitting on a chair?* Or, *do you have red hair?* Super obvious. One question needs to have a *yes* answer and the other question needs to have a *no* answer.

⋖⋖⋖ ⋗⋗⋗

THE YES / NO TEST

Once your helper has the questions ready and you are relaxed, close your eyes.

Breathe.

Relax.

Your body should feel completely at ease, with no sensations anywhere.

Have your helper ask you the *yes* question.

Immediately, you should feel a sensation or a change somewhere in your body. This is your *yes* response.

Have your helper ask you the *no* question.

Immediately, you should feel a different sensation somewhere in your body. This is your *no* response.

Perhaps you don't feel any sensations, but you instead have a strong inner knowing of *yes* or *no*. This is your response! Or perhaps you feel a sensation for your *yes* response but feel nothing at all for your *no* response. This is perfectly fine and very common.

Did you not have much luck on the first go? Then ask your helper to prepare another set of questions and try it again. But please don't be too hard on yourself! This one takes practise. It took me around twelve months to really get the hang of this.

Once you have mastered your *yes* and *no* responses, you can use this technique for literally any question that you may have about yourself and your life. Through using this technique, you are communicating with your soul energy by feeling the answer.

Now this technique is great, but it won't be effective if you are trying to use it while feeling emotional or upset or angry. These emotions get in the way of you being able to feel your *yes* or *no* response and it can often make the situation worse because the connection is blurred, which can make you feel even more upset. So please only use this technique if you are feeling relaxed and calm, particularly if you are still practising.

PENDULUMS

Pendulums are those incredible little tools that consist of either a crystal or some other small, solid object attached to the end of a length of fibre (string or cotton are common) or a length of chain. By using an external object to connect with your soul energy, it can often make the messages easier to receive.

You can buy pendulums from most businesses who sell crystals – you will know it's a pendulum because it will have a length of chain attached to the crystal. You can also make your own.

I recently went to a craft shop and purchased some beads with holes through the centre of each one. I tied a length of cotton approximately twenty centimetres long to a bead and there was my pendulum done!

Before you use your pendulum, you need to charge it with your energy. If it's a crystal pendulum, you'll want to cleanse the energy of the crystal first, so refer to the section of this book on crystals for tips on how to do this.

To charge your pendulum, close both your hands over it, close your eyes and imagine that the energy of your heart and soul is pouring into the pendulum. It really is as simple as that!

Now your pendulum is ready to use. Let's say you're using a pendulum made from a bead. Hold the thread end of your pendulum between your fingertip and thumb, so the bead is dangling from the other end. You can either rest your elbow on a solid surface or hold your arm in the air.

As you relax and breathe, focus your attention on the pendulum. Now ask your pendulum some basic and obvious *yes* and *no* questions, just like what your helper asked you in the previous technique. As you ask each question, wait for the pendulum to respond.

It will start to move in a specific way; it may swing from side to side, or backwards and forwards. It may spin in a circle, either clockwise or anticlockwise. Pay attention to how the pendulum moves with each question, and you can then determine your *yes* and *no* responses.

Pendulums can come in handy when emotions are running high and you need another way to connect with your soul-self, because you just aren't feeling the answers within yourself.

THE SWAY TEST

The Sway Test is a technique I learned after I realised that pendulums weren't my thing. Don't get me wrong! Pendulums are an incredible tool to use to communicate with the soul-self and I know many people who successfully use pendulums all the time.

But after playing with pendulums for a while, and getting frustrated because I just couldn't connect with mine the way I wanted to, I turned to the Sway Test. The Sway Test is the name I have given this test because, well, you sway!

Let me walk you through it, by using an example:

Some days my body can tolerate blueberries, and other days it can't. Mostly, my intuition – via my gut instincts or inner knowing – will tell me whether I should or shouldn't eat something but sometimes that inner knowing can be a little hazy.

When this happens, I turn to the Sway Test.

THE SWAY TEST

I hold a blueberry or two against my sacral chakra (just above my navel) with both hands. There isn't a precise spot here, anywhere between the naval and base of the sternum is fine.

My feet are shoulder width apart, so my stance is stable.

I close my eyes.

> I take a long, slow inhale through my nose. Hold.
>
> I then push the breath out through my mouth in a strong, long huffing motion.
>
> It is during this exhale that my body will do one of three things: either stay still, sway a little forward, or sway a little backward.
>
> If I stay still, it is neutral – meaning it doesn't matter whether I choose to eat the blueberries or not. If I sway forwards, it is positive – meaning at that moment, my body needs the blueberries (energetically and nutritionally). If I sway backwards, it is negative – meaning at that moment, my body doesn't need the energy and nutrients contained in the blueberries.

So what exactly is happening here? You are a giant pendulum! Your soul energy is giving you your answer via the movement of your body.

Some practitioners consider this a form of muscle testing – the muscles in the body are communicating with the soul energy, resulting in the physical response. Some people perform muscle testing using just your arm muscles; if the arm is strong and can hold when pressure is applied, it's a *yes* response and if it becomes weak against the applied pressure, it's a *no* response. This testing style needs a second person, to apply pressure to your arm, so I find it much more convenient to use the Sway Test.

This is my go-to technique for many things. I use it for food often, because I do have some food intolerances and I now know that my body has thresholds for how much of certain foods it can tolerate, before it becomes an issue. This test helps me determine whether my body is feeling overloaded with a particular food or not; as in, should I eat it or not.

I also use this test to help me choose which essential oils I'm going to put in my diffuser or in my massage oil, or to help me get a clearer answer on my *yes / no* response if I have an issue I'm struggling with or an important choice to make and my emotions are high. You could use this test for pretty much any *yes* or *no* question or problem you are facing.

Say you are looking at buying real estate and you have found a great little investment, but you aren't quite sure whether it's the right investment for you. Write the address down on a piece of paper, while holding the intention that you will buy the property, hold the paper to your body – just as I did with the blueberries – and do the Sway Test.

If your body sways forward towards the paper, the answer is *yes* – you should buy that property. If you move away from the paper, the answer is *no* – you should not buy that property. If you don't move at all, the answer is neutral – it doesn't matter whether you buy or don't buy, it will work out just fine either way.

Teach your children how to do this test! My children and I had a fun afternoon doing the Sway Test on ourselves. We had all sorts of food, essential oils and crystals lined up on the kitchen bench and we took turns testing them all. The results were really surprising! Sometimes, when we expected to have a certain response, our body moved in the opposite direction.

These techniques are you connecting with and working with your intuition. Pick one that you are feeling drawn to and have some fun with it. If you find that you are trying a technique and you just aren't getting the hang of it, don't feel disheartened. Let that one go for now. You can come back to it later. If you are struggling with all three techniques, I suggest giving them another go once you have finished reading this book because you will have a much deeper knowledge of all things energy and of ways to connect with the energy in and around you.

On the other hand, if you are having some success with any of these techniques now, go for it! Use it often, because what happens when you practise regularly? You become better at it.

By practising using your intuition with these techniques, you are strengthening your connection to your soul energy. And when you have a strong connection to your soul energy, amazing things happen! You will procrastinate less and you will find your confidence. Work that *inner knowing* muscle of yours as often as you can, because it will bring you so much strength and happiness.

KEEPING IT REAL

There is an important thing to note – please don't get too hung up on trying to find the right answer to every single question and decision you will have throughout your life. Case in point: I had a big decision to make a couple of years ago; I had a choice to make, and both options meant significant change. I was so upset and worked up over not knowing what to do.

My emotions were too high, therefore my connection to my soul-self was weak and my intuition was flat-lining and at this stage, I didn't know about the Sway Test and I struggled with the pendulum. I was so hung up on getting the right answer from Spirit, that it ended up causing me more harm than good – my eczema flared up until the itching and soreness drove me crazy and cold sores erupted like nasty little volcanos on my face. I was getting really annoyed with Spirit, for not speaking loud enough for me to hear over the mess of thoughts and emotions taking over my body.

Eventually, after twenty-four hours of zero sleep, not eating and being majorly stressed out, Spirit had had enough of my shenanigans and my soul-self bellowed at me, during a desperate attempt at meditation, *'It doesn't matter! Just choose whichever one you want to. Both options are viable, either way it is going to work out just fine.'*

Oh. Okay then. So, feeling a little embarrassed yet humbled, I made my choice. This choice did create big changes in my life and then a whole load of good things started coming my way. It came to me in droves.

Within a couple of days, I had some new, soulful and kind friends, my financial burdens lessened, my health and happiness returned, my family seemed happier and more united. It was like the flip of a coin as to how quickly things turned around for me.

Had I chosen the alternative option, I am certain things would have worked out similarly. Had I not been so hung up on getting the right answer or making sure I was doing the right thing, I would have saved myself so much worry and heartache. Sometimes, there is no right or wrong answer; there are just different options, all great in their own unique way.

Another thing worth mentioning: sometimes no matter how experienced you are at hearing your soul-self, you will misinterpret the signals and messages from time to time and things will go wrong. Don't sweat it! Your life isn't meant to be perfect in every way and you are meant to make mistakes. It's these mistakes that teach you the lessons that the Universe is sending your way.

There will also come a time when you listen to your soul-self and you will do exactly as it asks, and things still go wrong. I repeat: you are meant to make mistakes. You were given that message so things could go wrong, so you could learn the lesson. There is always a reason.

At the time, it will frustrate you beyond words (believe me, I've been there a few times) but once it's all said and done and the dust has settled and you eventually have time to look back and reflect, you will see that it all played out just as it was meant to.

Oh, and one more thing: these intuition exercises must be delivered with a word of caution – they can become highly addictive! The only time this may become a problem is if you become too dependent on getting an answer to your problems from someone or something else.

Yes, use these tools often, but don't become highly dependent on them because this can create a whole range of new issues for you. You want to use these tools to enhance your life, not to take over and run your life. Always remember, you are in control. If you ever feel like you have handed full control of your life over to someone else – even to Spirit – it's time to stop and reassess.

I am telling you all of this, not to make you lose heart and not to make you doubt your soul-self. I am telling you all of this to keep it real. To keep your feet planted firmly on the ground.

There is no magic formula for living a 'perfect' life. Being highly tuned to your soul-self will transform your life, but you still need to make mistakes and learn lessons and grow organically. It's all part of the journey! So please don't lose hope if you encounter any disappointing experiences (spiritual, or otherwise). Keep going! Chalk these disappointments up as life lessons and keep moving forward.

Once you are on track with your own intuition, I highly recommend teaching your children how to do it too. My two young children have become quite confident in connecting with and listening to their intuition through using the three techniques from this chapter. Children, in general, are incredible little humans who are very adaptable, accepting and eager to learn.

Imagine if you had been armed with this tool when you were a child and you grew up with your connection to your soul-self strong and clear! Being intuitive instils confidence and a deep sense of peace within. Don't deny yourself of this gift you were born with. Work with it. Trust it. Learn to trust in yourself. The more intuitive you become, the more you will *love yourself*. The more you love yourself, the more capable you will be of *sharing the love*.

8

LOVE

'you are absolutely deserving
of your own love.'

Love is a feeling. It is a smile. A hug. A kind word. Love is happiness. Love is inner peace. Love can't be measured, but we all feel it and know of its existence. Have you ever been in love? How did it make you feel?

Did you feel scrumptious tingles deep inside you? Did it vastly improve your mood? Did you feel a calmness settle over you? Or perhaps you felt like you had tremendous volts of electricity coursing through your body, feeling like you may explode in an array of brilliant stars at any minute! Has love ever made your heart feel like it was literally swelling inside your body from pure joy?

All these feelings are an energetic reaction. In a spiritual sense, positive energy is pure love. We expose our soul energy and our body to positive energy, and they respond. Imagine what can be achieved if we all start intentionally sharing love! The possibilities are limitless.

My motto is simple: share love as far and wide as possible. I believe this is the only way to true happiness and harmony. The more love that is spread throughout our world, the better our world will be.

LOVING YOU

But you must start with yourself. If you don't love yourself, then you won't have the reserves needed to share with others. If your metaphorical cup is empty, you can't pour from it. And if you keep pouring from a full cup without refilling it, the cup will soon empty.

You must love yourself fiercely and consistently. Practice self-care. Be selfish sometimes – it honestly is okay! As I write this chapter, I am sitting in a little cottage by the ocean tapping away on my keyboard, all by myself. I have a loving husband and two beautiful children, and I love them all deeply and unconditionally and they love me. But right now, I am taking this time to focus on myself. To loving myself. To caring and understanding myself. I am learning more about myself. It's only two days and my family are coping just fine! In fact, this is also an opportunity for them to reconnect and spend time together with a different family dynamic.

When I first thought of the idea to go to the coast for the weekend, I initially tried to find some friends to come with me. I felt like I needed other people with me, for my weekend away. But no matter how hard I tried, I couldn't find a single person who was available that weekend.

For a fleeting moment I felt disappointed, but that feeling disappeared just as quickly as it came. I then realised, this is just as it was meant to be – me, only me.

Never before in my life have I felt the need to be alone, and I have certainly never felt thrilled at the thought of it. Up until now, I associated being alone with being lonely.

It was time for me to end that association. Time now, to get to know myself and enjoy being with *me*. It's time to fall madly in love — with me.

I packed my laptop so I could work on my book, I packed my all-time favourite movies, favourite novels, favourite food and wine, favourite clothes, favourite activities like Sudoku and crosswords books (yes, I'm a puzzle nerd!) and I packed my yoga mat. I put a full tank of petrol in my little car, and I hit the road.

The playlist of my favourite songs I had put together the night before was now pumping out of my car stereo. My mood was ecstatic, as the familiar music filled my ears. My heart (almost literally, I swear) expanded with so much happiness from listening to my favourite songs one after the other, that the tears would well in the corners of my eyes and the feeling of bliss was almost too much for me to bear. And that was just the car ride!

I spent the next two days of my little get-away all loved up, just me and my favourite things. I binge-watched my movies as I sipped on my wine. I ate whenever I felt like it and not a second sooner. I lay on the beach, listening to the mesmerising hum of the ocean, breathing in the salty fresh air as I read my favourite book. I did many healings on myself and had many deep-and-meaningful chats with Spirit.

I dedicated many hours that weekend to writing; I was in the perfect place, geographically and spiritually, to find my creative flow and the words were spilling out of me and creating beautiful scripts on the pages. I slept deeply. I gave myself permission to heal on so many layers, that weekend.

Two days later and I was travelling home, feeling energized and blissful. I couldn't wait to see my family and I was ready and raring to face whatever life had in store for me from that moment on. I needed those couple of days to replenish my cup. And upon my return to my everyday life, my cup was then able to overflow to not only those whom I love the most, but to everyone else I encountered as well.

Take care of you, and the rest will follow. I am still learning how to love myself unconditionally and how to take extra special care of myself. It is not an easy thing to do, after many years of self-loathing, self-pity and self-destruction. But I am heading in the right direction – this is a monumental ride! If I can do this, so can you.

How much do you love yourself? I want you to ask yourself this question, right now. Is there room for a little or a lot of improvement in the self-love department?

PRACTICING SELF-LOVE

I want you to think of one thing that you love about yourself. Was that easy to do? Great! Was it difficult to do? Couldn't you think of even one little thing? You are not alone. There are many others out there who can't think of anything they love, or even like, about themselves. But you aren't going to give up because you are fierce. And you are stubborn. Put that determination to good use!

A child doesn't learn to walk as soon as they leave their mother's womb. It takes practice, determination, instinct and skill. You are now going to use practice, determination, instinct and skill to learn to love yourself. And if you do already love yourself, there is no harm in learning to love yourself more.

Are you kind? If you are reading this book, I can guarantee you are a kind person or at the very least you have displayed sporadic acts of kindness on and off over the years. If you don't think you are a kind person, call someone who loves you and ask them if you are a kind person. I bet they say yes!

You show kindness to others. Now think about that for a second. You show kindness to others. That is a big deal! Kindness is love. You are spreading the love to others, and that is a beautiful thing to do.

Put the mantra on the following page on repeat for a few days, or even a few weeks. Say it in your mind, all the time. Be patient. Be persistent. Be consistent.

The 'I Love Me' mantra takes seconds to say, and the benefits are huge. You can substitute *kindness* for any other trait that you love about yourself.

⋠⋠ ⋡⋡

THE 'I LOVE ME' MANTRA

Tell yourself, right now, that you love yourself for being kind to others. Seriously – right now. Say the words out loud, *'I love myself for showing kindness to others.'*

Then say it again. And again.

I love myself for showing kindness to others.

I love myself for showing kindness to others.

I love myself for showing kindness to others.

⋠⋠ ⋡⋡

As you persist with this mantra, are you noticing any subtle little changes in yourself as the days or weeks go by? Maybe you are starting to feel a little less sceptical, or you are feeling a little happier than before. Maybe you have started to notice something about yourself that is wonderful, and you hadn't noticed it before.

What is happening here? You are acknowledging that you love yourself, and your body and soul is responding with joy! If you aren't noticing any little changes, give it time. Remember: practice and determination. It is happening, you just haven't recognised it yet.

Now that you are getting in the swing of things, I want you to think of another thing that you love about yourself. Still stuck for ideas? Here are a few to get you started: you are helpful, you are compassionate, you are funny, you are nurturing, you are generous.

Have you noticed that all these suggestions so far have not been about your appearance? Your body will get its turn, but for now we are focusing on your soul – your personality. What makes you… you? Keep working on your own personal mantra of self-love. As your self-love list starts to grow, I promise you will notice a change in yourself.

Even the tiniest of changes are massive wins. So celebrate every positive change, no matter how small it may seem. This new-found love that you have for yourself will start to radiate outwards and others will notice the changes too. People who love themselves radiate a very special kind of energy, and it is contagious.

By now, you should have quite a few personality traits on your self-love list. It is now time to channel your love to your body – your temple.

LOVING YOUR BODY

Your body is your home. Your soul resides here in this temple, and your body works damn hard every minute of every day to support your soul. Your body uses an enormous amount of energy to do the simplest of functions like breathing and pumping blood. It is a machine that deserves respect and admiration.

Are you ill or injured? Then please take your focus away from the illness or injury and turn your attention to the positives about your body, for now. Is there something about your body that you don't like? Take your attention away from that, for now.

Pick one thing about your body that you love. And if you are struggling with this, it can be the tiniest of things. Here are some suggestions to help you get started: you have neatly manicured nails, you have strong cheekbones, your eyes are a beautiful colour, your hair is awesome, your freckles are cute.

Or how about going within your body: your heart is pumping blood through your entire body, your lungs are providing oxygen to your entire body, your eyes give you sight, your ears allow you to hear – you get the idea! Pick something, then start your mantra: *I love my body's ability to hear* or, *I love the colour of my eyes.*

Repeat this mantra all the time, every day, until you notice some more changes starting to happen. Then move to the next item on your self-love to-do list. Practice and determination.

At some stage you will eventually feel strong enough to tackle those parts of your body that you don't particularly like or aren't comfortable with. You might even find that by now, those body parts don't seem that bad after all! These are next on your hit list. Be gentle and kind with yourself. Show yourself compassion, like you would show to another person. Take a look at that body part (or if it is internal, think about that body part), imagining it was on someone else because you are your harshest critic. Look at it from a third-person perspective, because you would never think poorly of it if it were on, say, your friend's body.

Look at that body part with love. Project love and kindness to it and it will respond, and you will start to see it in an entirely new way. Thank it for all the hard work it has done over all these years, because it *has* worked exceptionally hard for you, despite what you may be thinking.

Your body is constantly communicating with you – sending you little messages. If it isn't functioning properly, it is trying to send you a message. If you can't bring yourself to send love to this body part just yet, then at the very least, thank it. Show it gratitude. That is a great start! Being thankful and showing gratitude are positive actions. And that is ultimately what we are aiming for – to channel as much positive energy as we possibly can via thoughts, feelings, words and emotions to our own body and soul.

It takes practise! Don't give up. You are a determined warrior and you are absolutely deserving of your own love. You are now committed to the act of self-love and nothing can stop you.

SELF-LOVE THROUGH INSTINCT AND SKILL

We have now well and truly covered practise and determination in achieving self-love. What about instinct and skill?

Let's talk about skills. We all have skills. What skills do you have? And how can you use these skills to help you on your journey of self-love? Do you have the gift of the gab? Then for goodness sakes, talk yourself into loving yourself. You can talk other people into pretty much anything, so you can definitely do this.

Are you an artist? Try painting or drawing a portrait of yourself, as you hold love in your heart. Are you super organised? Then get your diary out and pencil in every time that you are going to repeat your mantras. Add this activity to your schedule! Think of a skill that you excel at and then get creative – figure out a way to incorporate this skill into your self-love practice.

Let's now talk about instincts. We all have natural instincts, but many of us have lost touch with this incredibly powerful natural ability. We have already discussed intuition earlier in the book, but there is so much more to learn. Do you want more help with tapping into your inner instincts? Your intuition? Then you will thoroughly enjoy the section in this book on self-care.

In this later section dedicated to self-care, I explore many other ways you can get back in touch, and stay in touch, with your inner soul-self – your soul energy. I sometimes refer to this as a spiritual awakening. You can call it whatever you like: self-discovery, finding a faith, expanding your mind, growing, or simply learning.

By practicing self-care, you will learn how to listen to your inner-self and perhaps even communicate with it. Imagine that! Being able to ask your inner-self questions and not just rely on tools to help you with this – you will learn to hear or feel the answers *inside you.*

Believe me when I say, this is a *very* empowering experience and something I think everyone needs to learn how to do. Some people call it listening to their heart or going with their gut instincts. Whatever you like to call it – it is a very awesome tool to have on hand for things ranging from everyday decisions to major, life changing decisions.

All this talk about instincts and intuition is important because when you listen to your intuition and act on it, you are practicing self-love. The more you love yourself, the stronger your intuition becomes. And the more you listen to and trust your intuition, the stronger your love for yourself becomes.

I have communicated with my inner-self for everything from *what should I cook for dinner tonight?* and *which route should I take to work today?* to *what is causing my headache right now?* and even *should I stay in this relationship?*

I cannot stress to you enough how important it is to work on your intuition and your connection to your inner soul-self, so you can then love yourself on a deeper level. This internal compass is all yours and it is waiting patiently for you to connect with it. Use your soul compass to your advantage to help you navigate through your life journey.

SHARING THE LOVE

Now, let's get busy spreading that glorious love to everyone else. But remember, keep topping yourself up or you will be running on empty. How do you spread love? It doesn't take much – smile at someone, pay them a compliment, or my personal favourite, perform a random act of kindness.

Hug your loved ones; hold them close and hold thoughts in your head of sharing your love with them. Thoughts are energy, remember? Every time you have a thought about someone, it is channelling energy to that person.

There are thousands of random acts of kindness being performed all over the world every day, and most of them go virtually unnoticed. Just the other day, I watched some video surveillance footage shared on social media by a florist in the United Kingdom whose store had been robbed and vandalised. But the footage wasn't of the offenders who trashed his store. The footage he shared was of an unidentified man who walked past the store not long after the break in.

This anonymous man was out late at night with his friends, and he had left the party to go to the ATM up the road to get some more cash out and he was clearly in a hurry. He saw the mess on the footpath, of potted flowers that had been dragged from their pots and thrown all over the footpath and the road.

His automatic instinctual response was to gather up every single plant and gently place them back in the pots on the front of the store, where they belonged. This took him just seconds to do. Then he went on his way.

We aren't doing these things for attention or accolades. We are doing this because it is the right thing to do and it brings us an inner peace knowing we are spreading the love.

This man could have kept rushing past the florist's vandalised shopfront, like many people would have done. But he made a choice to help. And this decision touched the heart of the florist, who then went on a mission to track this man down to thank him.

That man wanted nothing in return. It was just the right thing to do. And this random act of kindness will, I am sure, forever stay with the florist and the original vandalism will be long forgotten. Love trumps everything.

LOVE AND ANGER / CONFLICT

Sometimes you will find yourself in a situation where the thoughts you are having about another person are far from positive. We are human, after all. When you do have a bad thought about someone, don't feel like you have done them an injustice. All you then need to do is send them love, before you move on. It takes seconds. Love cancels hate. Love trumps everything.

If you find yourself having negative thoughts about someone, try and remember that you are, in fact, sending them negative energy via these thoughts and this negative energy is not going to do either of you any good. When you are able, send them love. Think of that person, let's say her name is Candice, and say aloud or in your mind, *'Send Candice love.'*

And that's it. This is what I call, *sending a person unattached love* (which, by the way, is very different to being *in love* with someone). Sending a person unattached love helps all parties involved because you are a) releasing the negative energy that is likely gnawing away at you, and b) not projecting a whole lot of nasty vibes onto another person.

Whenever I have a huge fight with someone, or someone has said or done something that has deeply upset me, I get angry. Often, I'll curse and swear. I'll rant and rave a little bit, or a lot if I'm feeling extra mad. I'll say mean things to hurt them. In the moment, I'll have a whole host of negative thoughts and feelings towards that person (and perhaps towards myself as well, if the situation has triggered my old friend, self-loathing, again).

This is all how I can feel and act in a moment of extreme conflict. I don't make myself feel bad for reacting this way. Instead, when the heat of the moment has cooled down and I've had a chance to reflect, almost every single time I will then send that person unconditional, unattached love. Notice I said 'almost' – I'm getting better at it!

Do you know how *good* it feels to let that anger and emotion go? Such a relief! You don't need to be carrying around toxic energy all the time by letting your anger and frustration stew. You have better things to be focusing your energy on!

There will be some instances when you will find this exercise extremely difficult to do and some instances when you simply can't muster the strength or separate yourself enough from the heat of the moment to be able to do it at all. That's okay! Do your best.

No one is perfect; all you can do is try your best to be as loving and genuine as you can, as often as you can. You'll soon learn to recognise those people who are also loving and genuine, and those who still have quite a way to go. The more love you give to yourself, the easier it is to deal with and move through conflict. I promise!

All this talk of sending love to help conflict is not the same as being *in love* with someone. I am not suggesting that you be in love with someone who treats you badly; you are not a door mat. This is not the kind of love that I am referring to here.

There is a big difference between being stuck in love with someone who is toxic for you and sending unattached conscious love. By the way, energy healing is fantastic for overcoming this issue. I send conscious love to most people I see on a daily basis, this doesn't mean I am in love with them or that I expect anything from them in return. It is empowering and makes me feel good.

Now, I know what you're probably thinking right now – *this is all easy for her to say! I can't just stop loving this person, even though I know they are treating me terribly.* I hear you. And you're right; you can't suddenly decide one day that you're not going to love that person anymore.

It takes time, but the crucial key to moving on from a toxic relationship is this: love yourself more. The more you love yourself, the stronger and more resilient you become. Turn your attention to you. Do more of the little everyday things that make your heart sing; read your favourite books, watch your favourite movies, eat your favourite food. Check out the Joy List exercise at the end of this discussion for some further inspiration. Spend more time with friends, family and acquaintances who make you feel truly loved and appreciated! There are bucket-loads of these people out there!

Make it your personal mission to treat yourself like the lovable, kind and caring person that you know you are. If you aren't doing these things for yourself, no one else is going to do them for you. If you *are* doing these things for yourself, you are sending a message to the Universe that this is what you deserve and this is what you expect and, remembering like attracts like, the toxic people will slip away from you and more genuine, truly caring and loving people will come into your life.

So, you see, you don't have to figure out a way to switch off your love for someone who isn't right for you. You simply need to shift your focus. Focus on *you* and, given time and lots of self-care and perhaps embarking on your spiritual journey, you will soon realise that your feelings towards that person have changed and you can then set yourself free.

I have found that if there is someone hurting me or being toxic, this is all the more reason to send them conscious love. I have found that one of two things will then happen: said person's toxic behaviour miraculously ceases, or this person in one way or another exits my life. I have lost count of how many times I have put this theory to the test and it works every time, particularly when I combine it with the acknowledgement of the lesson I am being taught.

Love trumps hate. If I hated someone because they hated me, we would be going around and around in circles because like attracts like. It is a hamster wheel of negative energy that neither person can disembark. If someone upsets you or hurts you it's okay to be angry, but then move through the anger and let it go, as best you can. Throw a sprinkling of love into the mix and it changes the energy. Don't believe me? Try it! You will be pleasantly surprised. You can get off that hamster wheel and move on. You have that power. You are in control. And no one can take that from you.

THE JOY LIST

Here is a little exercise to help bring more joy, and therefore more love, into your life: write yourself a list of all the things, big and small, that bring you joy. Make it your mission to add more items to this list as you think of them. Then get busy doing everything on that list.

Do you love to sit quietly and sip on a cup of freshly brewed hot, sweet tea? Then do it!

Do you love to lay in the bath, with a glass of wine in hand, listening to your favourite music? Then do it!

Do you love to write poems? Then do it!

It is empowering to create your joy list. It will remind you of the little things that you often forget about when you are in the throes of being busy. You will recall things from when you were younger that used to bring you joy, that you haven't done for a very long time. This activity is a powerful act of self-love and you will feel the effect it has on you almost immediately.

I believe love is the single most effective superpower that we possess. As often as you can, bring your thoughts back to a place of love and you will flourish. Like attracts like, so keep projecting all those love vibes out to the world and it will come back to you tenfold.

I believe that everyone's soul purpose is to love, learn and teach. If we can all strive for these three things in life, we will have such a good time while we are here on Earth!

9

EGO

'Don't let ego get in the way of
being the best version of yourself.'

Ego (noun): A person's sense of self-esteem or self-importance.
I feel it is important to have an understanding of what ego is and how it works, so you can recognise it and learn to put ego back in its box when necessary. When I refer to ego, I refer to an expanded or extended version of the traditional definition of ego. I like to think of ego as the arch nemesis of soul energy. Without ego, we can't fully appreciate soul energy. So let's take a look at ego.

Ego is that smug part of us that tends to take over our thoughts and feelings, if we allow it. I was taught years ago, that if I act from a place of ego I will not achieve any success. That if I act out of ego, I will always find myself falling short of my dreams and goals. And if I act from a place of ego when I do healings for other people, my work will be inaccurate and ineffective. Confidence can sometimes be mistaken for ego – be mindful not to confuse the two. Intellect is another trait commonly confused with ego. Confidence and intellect are two wonderful qualities to possess.

Ego is that annoying little voice in your head that spurs you on when you know you are making a bad decision. Ego makes you feel like you need validation for doing something, rather than just doing it because a) it brings you happiness, or b) you are spreading the love.

There are far too many people in the world today who act from a place of ego, and it isn't pretty. Greed is a big one. Why are we all being so greedy?

As an example, there are so many gifted healers and psychics out there who truly do have a gift; they are not the con artists many people make them out to be, but they can't help others because they are coming from a place of greed.

They are so focused on charging extortionate prices for their services, then arrogance and greed creeps in and suddenly, they aren't as on-point with their healings or readings as they once were and the public labels them a fraud. Drop the ego, let love shine through and watch for the shift.

Is your desire to be liked by many people? Spread the love and be your true self – the right people will then be drawn to you.

Is your desire to have more money? Work from a place of love, not greed. Value your worth, give as much as you receive, and you will get your financial abundance. It may not come to you in the way you anticipate, but more on this later.

I am constantly silencing my ego. It is always going to be there lurking, but now I have control instead of ego controlling me. There have been countless times over the years where I have heard stories of very sick children, or communities who have been touched by tragedy, or someone has gone missing, and often my first thought is, *'I need to fix this!'*

But that is my ego speaking out. It is my ego making demands, bossing me around and getting all high and mighty. My thoughts almost automatically go into overdrive, as my mind madly scrambles to find a solution to make it all better. But I can't fix everything, nor is it my responsibility to do so. And if I make all this my responsibility, I will over-burden myself and it will all become too much to bear. And all this will take place, thanks to ego.

My ego tells me that I can and should fix, cure and heal everyone. My ego also tells me that I am better than other healers and, at times, has told me that I am not a good enough healer. My ego is wrong, on all accounts.

I had a conversation with a client recently who expressed her feelings of frustration and sadness over people in her social circles who were constantly competing with her in all aspects of her life. This competitive nature is extremely prevalent today, and it is doing a whole lot of harm to those on the receiving end and to those on the giving end.

Why is it important to be the best, have the most money, have the strongest relationships? Does it matter? Can't we just be satisfied that we are all doing the very best we can, to the best of our individual abilities?

We need to embrace our differences and rejoice in our shared likenesses. Support, don't compare. Be competitive, but be gracious and humble. Sprinkle kindness and compassion in with your determination, and watch it gain momentum.

If you find yourself competing with other people, or comparing yourself to them, there is a good chance that your ego has control of you. You therefore need to take back control and keep ego in check. How do you do that? Connect to your soul energy, to your heart centre.

This is essentially what this book is all about; to encourage you to go on a journey of self-discovery, to bring more happiness into your life and then ego has no other choice but to take a back seat.

If you find others competing with you or comparing themselves to you, send them unattached love. Because if they are behaving in this way, they have lost control of their ego and one of the quickest and most effective ways to help someone is to send them love.

Your reaction to their actions feeds the driving force, giving them strength and greater control. In other words, you can make the choice whether you feed their ego or feed their soul. Choose love, every time.

Don't let ego get in the way of being the best version of yourself. Ego may give you instant gratification, but it is short lived and it is addictive, so you will find yourself going back to it for more and more. Leave all that nonsense alone! Do everything from a place of love and you will find true happiness, and you will be free.

10

LIFESTYLE BALANCES: CHOICES AND CHANGE

'Make the decision right now, to turn your life around for the better.'

Every single choice we make is sending the Universe a message. And sometimes without realising it, the choices we make hold us back from bigger and better things. If your life is in turmoil and you aren't making any changes, then you have made the choice to stay and live in turmoil. Sometimes we get stuck in situations and we feel trapped; like we have no choice.

I am here to tell you that you always have a choice. You could make the choice to stay in the same situation, without making any effort to make a change. Staying put is a choice. Not being open to change is a choice.

Instead, you could choose to make a phone call to a friend for help. You could choose to start actively job-hunting because you hate your current job. Perhaps you will choose to spoil yourself for one day – just one day! – because you feel physically and emotionally drained from supporting everyone else in your life.

You may choose to turn off your mobile phone for an hour, a day, or longer so you can have some *me* time without distraction. The choice is yours.

BELINDA'S STORY

Here is a story to demonstrate the power of choices, and how the decisions we make can affect every aspect of our lives by either keeping us stuck in the same spot, or by generating change. This is based on the true story of someone dear to me, so I have witnessed much of what is described in this story. I watched someone I love go from being happy, to miserable, to happy again and the only thing that contributed to this was choices and change.

Not only did they learn some massive lessons on choices and change, I learned them too. And now I would like to share this story with you, to encourage you to be brave enough to make those tough choices and face change head on.

Belinda works as a retail assistant at a popular clothing chain. She has been working in that same shop for a couple of years and she applied for this job because it was her dream job and she told the store owner exactly this during her interview for the position. This job suited her bubbly and bright personality, her love of fashion, and her love of people.

In the beginning she was enthusiastic, dedicated, eager to learn, punctual and she was super-friendly to all the other staff and customers. In time, she made some strong connections with two other staff members and ended up becoming the best of friends with them. These three ladies spent lots of time together out of work hours; they would go away for weekends together, having the best times.

They were always calling each other or sending funny text messages back and forth. They confided in each other when they were feeling down or needed someone to talk to. Belinda was blissfully happy! Life couldn't get any better.

As the months went by, Belinda started to feel little tinges of frustration at work. Little things were starting to bug her. She dismissed these persistent feelings and kept working hard, pushing herself to keep up her enthusiasm and dedication to the job. Every day, it got a little harder.

She was starting to have silly little arguments with a couple of the other staff members and she was finding herself counting down the hours until knock off time. It was starting to sink in now; she was not loving this job. But this was her ultimate dream job! She had wanted this job so badly, and in the beginning it was amazing, but she was now struggling to remember what it felt like to wake up and be excited about coming to work.

If it weren't for her best friends also working there, she wasn't even sure if she could muster the strength to go to work every day. On top of this, she was having these strange, inner thoughts about working for the opposition chain on the other side of town. Thoughts that she'd tossed around from time to time over the years. They popped in and out of her head like delicious little daydreams.

This other fashion house, Belinda told herself, was only that – a dream. It could never be a reality; they would never employ her. She wasn't classy enough or savvy enough. So she pushed those thoughts away, rejecting them with scorn.

As the months continued to tick by, Belinda started to resent her job and most of the people she worked with. The customers were even annoying her! She usually adores her customers – what on earth was going on?

Belinda's health started to deteriorate and she was starting to have the odd sick day here and there, which was very out of character for her. She was bringing her work frustrations home and was taking it out on her family. She was short-tempered and tired all the time; not her usual chatty self. And she really, really hated her job.

She felt like she had no other choice but to continue working there because she needed the money. She felt obligated to stick it out, because this was supposed to be her dream job and her inner desire to work at the highly coveted opposition chain was completely unreasonable; what else could she do?

Belinda was actively choosing to stay in a bad situation. She felt like she had no choice, but she did have a choice. What message was she sending the Universe by staying put? She was saying that it was okay to stay there, so the Universe was obliging. There was not going to be a change, unless she allowed the change. Or unless the Universe played its hand and forced the change by throwing something massive Belinda's way.

Belinda had a chat to her friend one night, over a glass of wine, about her work frustrations and how badly it seemed to be impacting on her in so many ways. Her friend suggested she start job hunting because, what's the worst that could happen? She doesn't get any interviews. What's the best that could happen? She gets a new job!

Belinda's friend helped her realise that all is not lost. That she does have a choice beyond staying put. The other options are indeed scary, but isn't all change scary? Despite her current comfort zone being miserable, the thought of stepping out of this comfort zone frightened her. The thought of not being able to see what was ahead in her journey, that had up until this point been all mapped out and familiar and comfortable, was terrifying.

Belinda realised she had to push through her fear of the unknown. She knew she had nothing to lose, so she updated her resume and started applying for jobs she was feeling drawn to.

The fact that Belinda made a conscious choice to put her focus elsewhere, brought about some changes in her life. She didn't seem to be getting the flu all the time, like she used to. And she didn't feel quite so tired all the time. Belinda turning her attention to getting another job, sent a message to the Universe that she was ready for change, and the Universe was obliging.

Belinda now works for the company she originally thought was way out of her reach, and she is blissfully happy once more! It turns out that her fears of not being good enough were unfounded. It turns out, the managers of this retail chain were beside themselves with excitement over her application.

She adores her new job and she earns more money. She has a great boss and she works better hours. She still has her two best friends and things are falling into place. Belinda realised, upon reflection, there was a reason for everything that had unfolded in those past few months.

She realised she was meant to take that first job, because without it she would never have met her two best friends. She realised the purpose of that first job was to connect the three women and kindle their new friendships. And she realised this was the sole purpose of that first job. It wasn't serving any other purpose for her, once the friendships were established.

She realised that, had she trusted her instincts months ago, she could have saved herself a lot of pain and anguish. Had she trusted her instincts, she would have acknowledged that things weren't right and she would have pushed through her fear sooner and made a change.

She also realised that, although it was a very trying few months, she had learned many lessons – the biggest being: trust her instincts; those persistent little daydreams. And the other lesson: don't let fear of change cripple her!

Learn to read the signs from the Universe, because they are everywhere! The Universe was telling Belinda that it was time to move on, and her intuition was validating this same message, but she wasn't listening to either of them.

CHOICES AND INTUITION

Choices are presented to us all the time, every day. And who better to help us make these choices, than our own intuition? Can you see a pattern emerging here? Intuition is in the spotlight again! Intuition is our soul energy communicating with us. Our soul energy knows best, every time, without fail.

Sometimes, yes, we misinterpret what the message is but, as we've already learned, that doesn't mean we should ignore it or lose faith in it. Life is a special journey, and one where we will have many speed bumps along the way. But that's life – we learn from our mistakes, and we relish in the bliss of all the good bits.

As a healer and spirit communicator, I am often helping other people figure out the best way forward for them; providing them with clarity and confidence through the energy healing sessions, so they can make more informed choices. Sometimes the spirit messages seem confusing and my ego will occasionally step in for a second and say to me: *you can't send her away with a message like that. You haven't solved the problem for her!* But I am now very quick to silence my ego.

I allow myself to go back to my heart space where I can replay the message and then I am able to feel if it is the right message for that person, at that moment in time. If I get a comforting, peaceful feeling wash over me, I am happy to send that person on their way. This peaceful feeling is my intuition stepping up and giving me a helping hand. I am using my intuition to help others choose which path to take; which choice to make.

You can do this too! You may or may not be able to communicate with other souls, but you can absolutely learn to communicate with your own soul – after all, it is yours. Once you feel a strong connection to your intuition, let it guide you when making your own decisions. Practice and determination. You got this.

TOOLS FOR CHANGE

How can you bring about change in your life through the choices you make? There are some handy little tools that can help you with this! De-cluttering your life is a great self-care action and this is discussed in more detail later in the book. De-cluttering is also the act of making a change. The act of removing things from your life that are no longer necessary or needed is sending a message to the Universe that you are finally done with it and are now ready for new things to come your way.

These new things may be possessions, relationships, or life experiences. Sometimes you may not be entirely sure what new things you would like in your life and if that's the case, don't worry because I believe the Universe is an ever-knowing energy, and it will bring to you whatever it is you need at that particular stage of your life journey. All you need to do is trust that what comes your way is for your highest good and let the Universe and destiny and fate and *what will be, will be* take care of the rest.

VISION BOARDS

On the other hand, if you know exactly what you want, you need to introduce yourself to the concept of vision boards. These lovely little tools are an effective way of providing yourself with something you desire in your life.

You can create a virtual or a physical vision board. And you can put on this board whatever you like. I like to keep my vision boards focussed on one area or topic, but it won't matter if you scatter lots of random desires on the one board.

I was a self-employed bookkeeper before I discovered universal energy and spirituality. I owned my little bookkeeping business for about seven years and it was ticking along nicely, but I knew it was capable of more. At that time, my business was turning over around twenty-thousand Australian dollars per year and I had previously been happy with that because it was injecting a nice little bit of extra cash flow for my family.

Now however, I was determined to launch my little sole trader business into a big bookkeeping enterprise. I had just finished reading a book on manifestation and I thought it sounded like a fantastic way to boost my business to my visionary end goal I was fantasising about.

So off I go to my local stationery supplies store to purchase a cork board and some pin tacks. I laid the cork board on the floor of my loungeroom when I got home, dug out my kids' stash of coloured markers and pens, grabbed a fistful of A4 paper from the recycling pile in the box under my desk, and I got busy creating my vision board. These were the items I added to my vision board for my business:

- To employ another bookkeeper to take on the bulk of the work, so I will be free to work on my business and not in my business.

- To be turning over one hundred thousand Australian dollars per year.

- To complete my Certificate Level Four in Bookkeeping within twelve months and obtain my BAS Agent Registration.

- To have my business operating independently, so I can then be free to do other things.

- To have at least fifteen clients on the books.

- Less stress!

- More family time!

I then added some extras to my vision board to finish it off; some stars and a few smiley faces too – if I'm going to be looking at it every day, I want it to be cute. Then I mounted my board on the wall of my home office and stood back to admire my work. I had some huge goals. I had lots of work to do!

I had no idea how it was going to happen but I trusted that my vision board, combined with my positive thinking, would send enough positive vibes my business's way and enough messages to the Universe for it to all fall into place, somehow.

The next twelve months tick by, and I have now completed my studies and attained my Certificate Level Four in Bookkeeping and I have employed another bookkeeper to help reduce my workload. I had also managed to pick up an extra client. It was a lot of hard work, and without the support of my amazing husband I could never have managed to pull those first-year achievements off.

Year two rolls around, and I've had a couple of hiccups. There were some frustrating times – many lessons learned! The day I put my big girl pants on and took action on some things that had been plaguing me for months, was the day that everything started to fall into place. This was the day I pushed through my fear and soldiered on bravely, into the unknown.

I made a very desperate phone call to a bookkeeping colleague who was also a sole trader, to ask if she wanted some more work. It was a long shot, and I had a feeling she would say no, but I had to try. Those couple of minutes felt like I was on autopilot. Her name popped into my head from out of nowhere, and I immediately found her number and dialled as fast as I could, before my mind took over and told me to settle down and think it through.

As expected, she told me she couldn't take on any more work and my heart sank, but then she asked if I would like the phone number of a friend of hers who might be looking for some bookkeeping work. This helped my heart recover, ever so slightly.

Enter, the lady who turned my bookkeeping business around and gave me hope that things would work out in the end. She started with me the next day. I went from having zero options, to having a huge silver lining presented to me.

Suddenly, my little business took off. I had new clients coming out of my ears, and between the two of us we had things running like clockwork. It was fantastic!

My turnover had increased significantly, and I was working hard on my business; attracting new clients, establishing working relationships with local accountants, promoting my business. Before I knew it, I was a fully certified bookkeeper, I was a registered BAS Agent, I had one employee, I had fifteen clients on my books, and I realised I was looking at turning over almost one hundred thousand dollars in that financial year. And it all just kind of happened.

Yes, I worked extremely hard that year, but knowing I had ticked off most of my desires from my vision board was very satisfying. It was a whirlwind year.

It was during that same two-year period that I first learned of spiritual energy, so I was experiencing all of that on the side, as well as running my successful bookkeeping business. Things came to a head one day, when I realised I couldn't keep working on two businesses at once, so I had to make a decision. I had to choose between my two businesses – healing, or bookkeeping? I chose healing.

As soon as I made that decision, the final goals from my vision board fell into place. I sold my bookkeeping business to my employee and it was an effortless process – no fuss or drama whatsoever. Suddenly, I had boosted my turnover to being just over my target of one hundred thousand dollars. I had also removed the stress factor from my work and was now able to spend more time with my family. Oh, and my bookkeeping business was now running independently of me, I had generated a nice little income boost, and I was now free to do other things. Those last couple of goals weren't quite the way I had originally foreseen them, but they had happened nonetheless.

Every single thing on my vision board wish-list had been achieved! Sometimes, I had to put the hard yards in and work like crazy to get what I wanted. Then other times, things just happened without me having to do or say much at all. It was a combination of hard work, and trust in the Universe and in my own instincts, that saw my vision board come to fruition.

That is just one example of when I have used the help of a vision board to achieve success in my life. And I know of many other people who have used this tool with success, also. I am here to tell you that it works. And it's fun!

Vision boards are the epitome of visualisation techniques. They are visuals of what you desire, right smack bang in your face all the time. Every time you look at it, you are giving it energy and power. You are putting your visualisations down in hard copy, giving them substance. You are manifesting what you want in your life.

I use visualisation techniques every single time I perform a healing on someone. I use them in my own life, every single day – several times a day! I cannot emphasise enough how powerful our thoughts are; if I didn't use the power of my thoughts at times when I did healings, my healings would be nowhere near as effective. I visualise the energy of the Universe flooding me and pouring out of my hands and into my client. I visualise that same energy flooding the person's body, filling them with love and light.

This often results in me feeling the energy on a much stronger level, and often results in the client feeling huge sensations moving through their body. So put that amazing power you hold to good use and channel it to your vision board and to your deepest desires.

POSITIVE AFFIRMATIONS

My second favourite tool for bringing about change, is regular positive affirmations. These little beauties will help you manifest good things in your life. An affirmation is a declaration or a proclamation. Positive affirmations are positive statements that you say or think every day, and because your thoughts are energy, you are sending all that daily positive energy directly to the subject of the statement. Here is one of my favourite examples:

I am love. I am deserving of love and I effortlessly receive love from all areas of my life.

This little positive affirmation is sending a very powerful message to your own soul energy, your own body, other people, and to the Universe, that you are nothing but love. Everything you are is love. This is what you want and what you deserve in your life. By making this affirmation every day, you are fuelling the affirmation with lots of energy – it will magnify and quantify. It will become your reality.

I will briefly mention there is a flip side to positive affirmations. Negative affirmations. It is worth discussing, because you may be sending out negative affirmations and not realise it. If you can bring your awareness to what you are inadvertently doing, you can make a change.

The next time you catch yourself saying or thinking things like *my life sucks* or, *I hate my hair* or, *this food is so bad for me*, remind yourself that you are projecting negative affirmations out to the Universe and because you are sending lots of negative energy to those subjects, you are never going to achieve your desires. When you do make a negative statement, acknowledge it and then send love. Remember, love trumps everything. So, no matter what you do in life, no matter how many mistakes you make, always come back to love.

Positive affirmations will bring you joy, happiness, peace, harmony, fun and laughter, good times! They have the power to transform your life. They have the power to bring about huge and often unexpected changes in your life. Nothing but good things can come from working with positive affirmations. You are sending a very clear message to the Universe that this is what you desire.

Another brief reality check, if I may: sometimes for us to achieve our deepest desires and for us to come closer to what the Universe has in store for us, we need to go through changes or experiences that aren't pleasant. Sometimes, by manifesting a better life for ourselves, we are forced to travel through some rough patches. These low points in our life are an important part of the journey and the best thing we can do is pick ourselves up and keep going. Learn the lesson, remind yourself that this low moment in your life is temporary, and keep moving forward.

Some people may argue that these low moments disprove the whole concept of your ability to bring about positive change. They may say if you try and manifest something good, and something bad ends up happening, it simply didn't work.

I say to those people: look at the bigger picture. Change your perspective; cast your awareness wider than the problem you are being faced with.

I also say that the act of believing in something – of holding on to *hope* – is in and of itself sometimes more important than the outcome. If you do nothing else, at least hold on to hope and keep believing. It will give you strength you never knew you had.

Back to our positive affirmations. Here are some other little crackers that you might like to put on repeat, to bring about happiness in your life.

POSITIVE AFFIRMATIONS

'I have limitless abundance in my life, in all areas.'

'My community is a safe place; my neighbours are my friends.'

'I am ready for change. I do not dwell on the past.'

'I have a deep respect for and connection with Mother Earth. This land where I live is fertile, fruitful and healthy.'

'I possess all the wisdom and knowledge I will ever need. I connect with this wisdom through intuition and learning.'

'Peace surrounds me. I can feel it and I am also at peace.'

'I am successful in everything I do. I achieve my goals effortlessly.'

If you are interested in working with positive affirmations but are struggling to come up with your own, there is a huge selection available to you. There are apps you can download onto your mobile phone or electronic device, there are websites devoted to a plethora of positive affirmations. There are positive affirmations in print that are available to purchase, making a beautiful addition to your home or office décor. They are printed on t-shirts. They are all over social media!

You should have no trouble at all getting your hands on some positive affirmations that resonate with you. Once you have these little babies on your team, get ready for positive change to come your way.

OTHER WAYS TO BRING ABOUT CHANGE

Do you need some more suggestions to kick start a change in your life?

- *Research ways to reduce your debt and increase your cash flow.* The Barefoot Investor is a good place to start. Look him up online – and no, I am not working for him or with him in any way. I just love the way he works! I also love marketplace websites – being able to sell or give away all possessions you no longer need is very liberating. Especially if that possession is costing you money unnecessarily and you don't need or want it anymore. Get rid of it.

- *Figure out how you can reshuffle your day, to allow yourself some me time – every single day!* You should be your number one priority. You know that hour or so you spend on social media, scrolling mindlessly through news feeds every day? Scrap that and replace it with something you love to do. Or dedicate a day or two a week to being social media free. Then go for a walk! Catch up with a friend. Meditate. Read a book. Go get your nails done. Do something, do anything, for yourself!

- *Make time in your day to devote to your loved ones.* You need to be present. You need to keep the communication lines open at all times. Once the communication stops, relationships falter fast. If you are not being *in the moment* when you spend time with your loved ones, the connection with them becomes weak. Imagine, for example, your current relationship thriving because you chose to devote as much time to this as you did to those other new and exciting relationships emerging around you!

- *Think of an area in your life you are not happy with.* Now think about a change you can make to help that area become better and brighter. And if you can't think of anything you can do to make a change, refer to the notes in this chapter to help you out. If you still feel stuck, then at the very least, start each day with a daily affirmation like, *'I am open to change. I accept change for my highest good. The Universe will deliver; I am ready.'*

THE IMPORTANCE OF LIFESTYLE BALANCE

Finding a balance in your everyday life can seem tricky sometimes. You may even think that finding a healthy, happy life balance is impossible to achieve.

> *I don't have any time for myself anymore. All I do is work, look after the kids, study, keep the house tidy. I am too exhausted at the end of the day to be bothered doing anything of an evening. I feel so drained when I wake every morning; I try to get a solid night's sleep but sometimes I just don't have time to get to bed until midnight or after. I feel like I am on autopilot, just rushing through my life trying to pay bills and keep my family happy.*

Sound familiar? You are not alone.

The choices we are making today are putting enormous amounts of pressure on us. Some people have three jobs, just to pay the bills. Some people are trying to survive on three hours sleep each night. Some people are experiencing relationships falling down around them that might otherwise have thrived, had these relationships been given the time and energy they deserved.

Credit card debt is skyrocketing as we scramble to live a lifestyle that seems unsustainable. We are spreading ourselves dangerously thin, and the cracks are starting to show. Why are we even here? What *are* we doing with our lives? Are we living? Or are we simply existing?

What *is* the point to life?

I believe there must be a point, or we wouldn't be here. There is so much more to life than just paying bills and running yourself ragged, day in and day out. If this is you, it's time to sit down and brainstorm ways to bring about change to your life.

What is the point to life? Happiness! Happiness, love, relationships, adventures, lessons. Yes, life is hard. Sometimes, it's really hard. But the good should always outweigh the bad. We work hard, we strive for success, we achieve our goals, we have fun!

We learn, we love, we teach. I believe these are the crucial elements to happiness here on Earth. So, let me ask you: how can you make a change in your life for the better? Baby steps. One little change at a time, or you will become overwhelmed and will find yourself back in the old habits that have been getting you nowhere.

LETTING GO OF THE PAST

There is no point dwelling on the past, it has already happened. And there isn't a thing you can do to change the past. What you can do, is make peace with your past decisions and past choices that didn't go to plan so you can keep moving forward. Leave the past where it belongs. You may feel like it's not possible to let go of the past, no matter how hard you try and how desperately you want to let it go, but it is possible.

If there are repercussions happening now from past events or decisions, deal with them in the now. My favourite way of dealing with these things is by sending healing to whatever it is in the past that is still bothering or affecting you. It won't change what happened, but it will set you free.

Having past events still affecting me in my daily life was one of the reasons I started seeking alternative ways to fix myself – to be happy again. I knew I had to let it all go, I just didn't know *how* I was going to do it. At one stage, I didn't think it was going to be possible to move on from my past decisions, relationships and mistakes. I thought it was going to be something I had to deal with every day, for the rest of my life. Boy, was I wrong!

I went to a psychologist, which helped but didn't quite set me free. I went to a hypnotherapist, which helped but didn't quite set me free. I talked to my family and friends about it, which helped but didn't quite set me free. I wrote myself letters, which helped but didn't quite set me free.

I tried so many things. I was so angry with myself for not being able to let it go. I knew I *needed* to do it, but I *couldn't* do it. I now know that I was on the right track; all those things did help and I learned so much about myself along the way.

However, when energy healing and ultimately my spiritual awakening came into my life, I was transformed. My life changed in ways I never thought possible. One day, it dawned on me that those events from my past that had continuously haunted me for so many years, were no longer at the forefront of my mind. They had receded to the background of my thoughts, and I was finally free. I was at peace with my past; with those speed bumps that pulled me up in my tracks over the years gone by.

There will always be speed bumps along the way. These not-so-great days are inevitable. They come to us to teach us lessons. They come to us, to force change in our lives so that bigger and better things can come our way.

They also come to us, so we can experience the full range of human emotions. This human experience allows our soul energy to grow and expand. To learn. To evolve. Ride through the darker days as best you can, knowing that these times are temporary, and you will get through it. Keep reminding yourself there are better days ahead.

I encourage you to *please* make a choice right now, to bring more happiness into your life. You are a warrior! Practice and determination – remember? You can absolutely one hundred percent do this.

I believe in you. Your family and friends believe in you. The Universe believes in you. Now, it's time for you to believe in yourself. Make the decision right now, to turn your life around for the better. You are no longer going to coast through this life on autopilot. You are taking charge and you are going to get busy living!

11

LESSONS: NAVIGATING THROUGH THE SPEEDBUMPS

'Life's toughest lessons should not define you. Nor should they control you.'

Conflict
Sickness
Mistakes
Failed relationships
Flaws
These are all lessons.

In the midst of the lesson, life is hard. In the midst of the lesson, you feel like there is no end in sight. You feel like you will never climb your way to the surface to breathe. Not knowing the outcome is bloody scary. Not knowing which decision to make is scary. Feeling lost, and hurt, and confused, and angry, and sick challenges you to your core. You may not know the solution; how do you bring an end to these challenging times? But it's not the end that matters. What matters is how you get through it; how you *survive*.

So, the million-dollar question: How? How do you survive? *How* do you navigate the speed bumps? You survive, first of all, by reminding yourself that *this is temporary*. Even the good stuff is temporary; all of it will pass eventually. This situation that you are currently in, is not forever. It will pass, regardless of the outcome. It will pass and you *will* get to the other side, wherever that may be.

Comfort yourself with this knowledge. Reassure yourself, ask your loved ones to reassure you: *this will pass*.

How else do you survive? It's never black and white. There is no magic quick fix. I can however, share with you a little something based on what I have learned and witnessed. Trust that the Universe, or God or whatever higher power you believe in, has your back and remind yourself that these experiences are shaping you to be a better, stronger person. I guess you call it *faith*. Faith will get you through it.

And don't forget, you have that awesome superpower you can always rely on: *Your Intuition*. When you are faced with a choice, stop for moment and ask yourself, *'Is this right for me?'* and eventually, with practise, you will feel or simply know the answer. You will know whether to surrender and let go or whether to keep pushing forward.

Your intuition will get you through thick and thin. Good times and bad times. Keep trusting your instincts and being your best, authentic, happy, real self as often as you can, and the speed bumps then become easier to bear, even if just a little bit.

Seek support whenever you need it! Don't be afraid to admit defeat, or show weakness, or express your sadness, or even hatred. Ten years ago, my son's kindergarten teacher sat calmly with me and my son, while he was in the middle of a full-blown meltdown.

'He's okay. Just let him feel his feelings,' she said to me.

She didn't tell him to settle down. In fact, she couldn't tell him to settle down because he was so distressed, he wouldn't have heard her words. She didn't tell him he was doing the wrong thing. She didn't fuel his emotion with more emotion by getting angry and upset as well. We both sat with him, as he had his moment of sadness and frustration, until he was able to move through the emotion and come out the other side.

It only took a minute or two. He was exhausted, but he was supported and loved. And, most importantly, he had released all the emotion that had risen inside him.

Now I understand this parenting technique isn't for everyone and I certainly don't think it is appropriate to use all the time. But those very wise words of a young, yet experienced-beyond-her-years kinder teacher, have forever been ingrained in my memory and I find myself repeating these same words over and over – to family, to friends, to clients.

As often as you are able, feel your feelings. Every emotion is worthy of your attention so please, give all of them the respect they yearn for. Acknowledge your emotion. Sit with it a while. Watch, as it rises, then peaks and eventually falls. You're not holding onto it. You're not controlling it. You are giving it the space it needs, to move through you and into the never-never, changing you for the better as it goes.

Another tip that may help you the next time you find yourself in the throes of anxiety or a panic attack or any other powerful emotion: turn your attention away from your body's physical response and focus on the energetic reaction taking place.

This energetic reaction is happening for a reason – it is transforming your soul energy. Although it feels confronting and uncomfortable, breathe and welcome the energetic shift knowing that this is happening for a reason.

Don't focus on the cause, because this is simply a trigger to stimulate your own healing and lessons. When you consciously shift your focus to the energetic effect, you will find that you have a higher threshold for the experience. You will begin to see it for what it really is – a gift – an opportunity to heal and evolve.

Here is a great example: I was in a sauna with a friend and she was getting herself in a terrible state of anxiety over the heat. It was agitating her. It was making her sweaty and itchy. She was up and down, pacing around the small room constantly. She just couldn't settle and anxiety was beginning to take a hold on her.

Until I suggested she switch her perspective. When she stopped focusing on her body's physical response to the heat and began to instead focus on the *energetic interaction* taking place, her sauna experience was transformed.

She sat and breathed and felt all her feelings. She felt the waves of heat energy coursing through her body, transforming her own soul energy. She became calm and relaxed. She was able to sit for ten minutes in complete stillness, as she welcomed the energy healing she was experiencing.

She was able to immerse herself in the *entire* experience; making her physical experience much more tolerable.

Don't be afraid to feel your feelings! They are energy. You are energy. Acknowledging this can be comforting – it can help you through the tough times.

The tough times will teach you many lessons. When enough time has passed and you can look back on that hard time in your life, you will realise you have learned so much about yourself and your life during that experience. In the years I have been providing healings for others, I have never once heard a client say to me, 'I didn't learn anything from that tough time from my past.'

Every single person I have spoken to, who has surfaced from the other side of turbulent times, has openly acknowledged how it has, eventually, changed them for the better and how they have learned some huge lessons and how they are *grateful* for that experience. It's through these lessons that we can experience personal growth, which is a crucial element to living out our days here on Earth. If we don't grow, we sit idle. When we are idle, we miss out on so much!

Learn of the things you love, and don't love – by embracing new experiences. Learn of the values you hold dear – through past relationships; good and bad. Learn of your strengths, and of your weaknesses. Learn how to forgive – because not only does anger hurt the recipient, it mostly hurts you. Learn how to love – love yourself and love others passionately! Learn when to walk away – through making past mistakes. Learn how to connect with yourself on a deep and intimate level – through past sickness.

It all passes. Pay attention to the lesson so you can free yourself and move on.

It has taken me almost twenty years to learn some of my most valuable lessons. Now, I can look back on my past trauma and smile, but it took me a long time to get here.

Over and over and over again, I kept making the same mistakes. I was continuously frustrated and angry. I was too busy blaming everyone else for being horrible and inconsiderate people and didn't take the time to have a look at *myself*.

It took me twenty years to let that finger I had been indignantly pointing at other people, fall to my side. And the moment I stopped blaming everyone else for my pain – the moment I chose to look inside myself, to learn more about this pain – was the moment I experienced true healing and freedom.

My tender and young heart being trampled on and broken at age eighteen by an older man, was a lesson.

Watching my dad fade away and die from almost an entire lifetime of type one diabetes and eventually cancer, was a lesson.

Developing ulcerative colitis and my subsequent rapid health decline, was a lesson.

Making uneducated decisions with money, resulting in the loss of tens of thousands of dollars over the years, likely more, was a lesson.

My personal list of speed bumps big and small, has moulded and shaped me.

As they say – you get knocked down, you get back up again. And again. And again.

We are all here in this human experience, so that our souls can grow. Your soul needs to experience the full spectrum of emotions and the only way this is achievable is through human experience. Your soul needs to experience trauma and heartache and sickness and mistakes so your soul can *grow*. We are all energy, and this energy has a purpose: grow and evolve. Navigate your way through the speed bumps of life, knowing that you are growing and learning along the way.

Life's toughest lessons should not define you. Nor should they control you. Life is all about experiences – good and bad – big and small. How can we know true love, if we have never experienced hate? How can we truly appreciate abundance, if we have never experienced extreme loss? Yin and yang. Up and down. Black and white. This contrast gifts us with appreciation and understanding.

So, the next time you are faced with one of life's speed bumps, remember:

> Breathe
>
> Trust your instincts

> Watch for the lesson
>
> Reach out for help
>
> Trust the Universe has your back
>
> Feel your feelings
>
> Ride out the storm as best you can, knowing it is temporary
>
> And, most importantly: love yourself, fiercely.

Even if you can only recall one of these suggestions in the heat of the moment, it will help.

Return to love, as often as you can. You *are* love. You are *loved*.

12

'DEAR HUMAN, WITH LOVE'

Welcome to the mystical, magical world
Of Higher Beings and Light Workers,
Of soul energy and vibrations,
Gentle whisperings and soulful murmurs.

Please, take a moment to acquaint yourself
With this often-unseen eternal life force
That moves in and around you,
As you escape from your thoughts.

Pause.

Can you feel it? Can you see it?
It is there! Open your awareness,
Tap into your higher consciousness
And you will soon realise
Life is not fruitless.

No more waiting or procrastinating
You! Blessed soul
It is your turn, right now,
To break the societal mould.
Embark on this journey,
And you will soon discover
Every human is but a speck
In this grand old Universe.

You are, in fact, a luminescent fleck
Of light that shines oh so bright, forever more!
Watch your worries melt away
Into the abyss that is Life itself.

Peace and true happiness are yours.
Are you compelled?
Be brave enough to cast
Your net of awareness wider,
Further than you ever dared before.

For it is here, dear one,
You will find the answers.

'What is the meaning of life?'

'What is my purpose?'

The answer to that which you seek?

Love.

That is all
And that is enough.
I am love. And I am everywhere.

In the air that you breathe,
In the sun and the moon,
In the earth beneath your feet.
Return to me. Return to love.

Return to you, infinite light thereof.
'Welcome home,' whispers your soul,
'There is much to learn,
opportunities abound, trust in me, let go...'

13

MIRACLES

'My life, at that moment, took a massive turn.'

Do you believe in miracles? There are miracles happening around the world, every second of every day. What defines a miracle?

It is, according to the Oxford Dictionary, an extraordinary and welcome event that is not explicable by natural or scientific laws and is therefore attributed to a divine agency. So in other words, it is something that happens, when realistically it shouldn't have. Miracles have been described as 'an act of God' by those of religious faith.

Miracles present themselves in all shapes and forms. I believe we are all surrounded by miracles, big and small, every day. I want to use this chapter to share a couple of stories of miracles I have been blessed to be a part of, and I have no doubt I will be witnessing many more in this lifetime.

I hope that, if you don't already, you too will come to wholeheartedly believe in miracles like I do.

MY HEALTH MIRACLE

In November 2015, my health started to rapidly deteriorate. I was very new to energy and was still finding my way. I had already experienced so many amazing things, but my trust in myself and in the Universe was being tested, big time.

It was at this time, I started experiencing symptoms suggesting I had something horribly wrong with my bowels. So off I went for a colonoscopy.

The doctor told me the news: I had ulcerative colitis in my colon. He told me I would have to forever be very careful and cautious about what food I was eating. He told me I would be on medication for the rest of my life to control this disease. He told me that, in many cases, ulcerative colitis progressed to cancer, or at the very least, surgery, to have parts of the colon removed.

He threw some very grim statistics at me, none of which I can remember because my mind was a blur. As all this new information about my body being in grave danger started swirling through my mind, I looked him square in the eyes. 'I am going to heal myself,' I said.

I meant it. He knew I meant it. There was not a doubt in my mind that I would come out of this new venture with a clean bill of health. Determination kicked in. My doctor was super supportive and gave me many alternatives and options to choose from; I trust him completely.

The first thing I was advised to do, was to go on the medication to suppress my immune system. Ulcerative colitis is an autoimmune inflammatory bowel disease. My body's autoimmune defences were overreacting. In short, my body was attacking itself. And its autoimmune response needed to be dampened, before it did any more damage.

Here was our plan: I would go on the prescribed medication to get my autoimmune response under control. I asked that this be a short-term solution, and he was very understanding and accommodating. In the meantime, I would research diets that would help heal my body from the inside out.

I chose not to discuss my plan to heal myself with energy healing with my doctor, because I was scared of being criticized. I started the medication and straight away started researching how I could heal myself with food and with spiritual healing.

Boxing Day, 2015. My health starts deteriorating. It seems to be a bad flu, but my usually reliable go-to remedies aren't helping at all. The next day, the inside of my entire mouth and my throat are sore. A few days later, I am in excruciating pain. I have a very high temperature and my entire body is sore. I am weak. I just cannot function.

Off I go to my GP for a check-up. My doctor suspects tonsillitis and gingivitis, but he says his gut instinct tells him that my new medication is giving me some nasty side effects, so he sends me off for blood tests.

That night, my doctor personally calls me on my mobile. He tells me to stop taking the medication immediately and to get myself straight to hospital. He tells me that my body has not responded well to the medication.

Instead of the medication gently suppressing my immune system, it has completely obliterated it. My white blood cell count is next to none, essentially leaving my body without an immune system. I am completely vulnerable and exposed to all flus, viruses and germs and should I pick up even a common cold, it could kill me.

Not only do I have ulcerative colitis, with an inflamed and very angry colon and all the nasty symptoms that go with it, I now also have a body that is pretty much shutting down, with no defence in place against all the nasties we are all constantly exposed to.

Suffice to say, the New Year's Eve of 2015 was not going to be a fun one for me. But the lessons I learned in those next forty-eight hours were some of the biggest lessons of my life.

I went straight to hospital, where I was poked and prodded. The nurses struggled to get an intravenous line in my arm; my veins kept collapsing. Sepsis had taken hold of my body and I needed antibiotics urgently, to get the infections taking over my body under control. My doctors later told me that during this time, my condition was so serious that my life was on the line. I had a raging fever. I was vomiting and I was in terrible pain from my head to my toes. My fingertips hurt. My eyes hurt. Every inch of my body was hurting.

My beautiful husband was beside me, reassuring me and holding my hand but I could see the panic in his eyes. That was a very long night, for both of us.

I was moved from the Emergency Department of the hospital, to my own room on a ward. By now, it was the morning of the thirty first of December 2015.

The doctors told me it was now a waiting game. We had to wait for my body to recover and they anticipated it taking days or maybe even weeks before my body would bounce back.

There was also the issue of the ulcerative colitis still running amuck in my body, with no medication keeping it under control. We devised a new plan: rebuild my immune system, consider an alternative medication to control the disease, and keep working on my diet so I could heal myself from within. I also privately resolved to boost my energy healings on myself and work more on my spiritual growth.

Luckily, I had some gut-healing food already prepared at home, so my husband brought my slow-cooked soups and stews up to hospital. I kept them in the fridge and used these to nourish my body, as it began the recovery process. My entire family were all sending me lots of healing, positive thoughts.

Late that afternoon, the nurses had a shift change. At the nurse's station, a few short steps from the doorway of my room, there now sits a nurse who coughs and coughs and coughs. I am feeling thankful she isn't my nurse, because the last thing I need is her germs wreaking havoc on my defenceless body, but the nurses on the ward are all using the same desk, computer and phone.

Her coughing gets progressively worse. I hear the other nurses tell her how sick she sounds and her saying how she wishes she could go home, to sleep off the virus. My panic starts setting in and I lay in bed crying, desperately hoping that her germs don't reach me because without an immune system, I could end up in some serious trouble.

Early that evening, my nose starts to run. I call my nurse and let her know and I can see the concern on her face. Late that evening, I am woken from my sleep by my nose running like a tap. I feel congested and know it's the onset of a cold. A persistent cough has also started.

It clocks over midnight. Happy New Year to me.

Panic is starting to rise within me, gripping me with fear. Amidst this rising panic, my Spirit Guides interrupted me with a booming message:

JO CAN DO THIS. FIGHT!!

I remind myself that everything happens for a reason. Could that sick nurse be more than just a stroke of bad luck for me? I suddenly see my situation from a new, positive perspective and decide that the sick nurse is a prompt to get me healing myself quick smart.

I get myself comfortable, close my eyes and visualise my body producing lots of white blood cells. I spent an hour laying there in bed, in the middle of the night, watching my body pump out these beautiful, perfect little specimens of white cells. I could see inside my body. I could see, in my mind's eye, the white cells forming and multiplying, and it was a magical sight indeed.

The show ended, and I fell asleep.

4:30am on the first day of January 2016, I wake to discover that my nose has cleared. The cough has gone. The nurses are surprised! And I feel very grateful.

I knew I had begun to heal myself, and I resolved to keep returning to my special healing show, knowing that it was working. I believe I have the power to heal myself.

Not long after I wake, my Guides deliver another message:

> *Write a healing mantra and share it with your family and friends, so those who wish to, can say it too.*

I scramble for a pen and grab an old hospital meal order form; the nearest piece of paper to me. I take a deep breath and close my eyes. Words begin to erupt from the depths of my soul and spill onto the back of the scrappy, creased little menu:

> *The food Jo eats is healing her.*
> *The air Jo breathes is healing her.*
> *The love Jo receives from me is healing her.*
> *Jo has a strong, functioning immune system.*
> *Jo has a healthy, functioning gut.*
> *Jo's entire body, from the molecular to the spiritual level, is healthy and in sync.*
> *Jo is loved and supported wholeheartedly by me.*
> *I know that Jo is grateful for all her blessings and lessons through this journey.*

I had my mobile phone with me, so I decided to put a public post on social media describing all my adventures from the last few days. It was time for me to come out of the spiritual closet.

That post was a significant step for me; up until that time, I wasn't openly talking to anyone, apart from my husband and my aunty, about the magnitude of my spiritual growth or my spirit encounters.

I was about to put it all out there, in front of everyone who knew me – my friends, colleagues and acquaintances. I was so scared that people would judge me and call me crazy. But I took a deep breath and hit the post button. My story was out there, easily accessible for all to see.

Within minutes, the well wishes and healing messages and thoughts started pouring in. I couldn't believe my eyes! There were so many friends sending me messages of support and encouragement. They believed me! They didn't think I was crazy! I felt empowered and strong.

I knew I was going to beat this, and fast. I kept on with the healings and kept repeating my mantra, using the support of those around me, combined with my own determination, to spur me on. The visions of my perfectly formed white cells became more vivid with every healing, until eventually it was as vivid as watching a show on a television screen.

Later that morning, the sick nurse – who was now much worse than the previous day – walked into my room. She found me happily sipping on my homemade soup, about to watch my magic show of white cells do their thing again.

Early that afternoon, more blood tests are done and the results come back. The doctor walked in my room, shaking his head in confusion. He tells me I have had a 'phenomenal increase in white cells' and I am almost within the normal range, and can go home immediately!

My life at that moment took a massive turn. I went from being frighteningly ill to relatively healthy, extremely happy and discharged from hospital within forty-eight hours. My family were by my side, supporting me. We were united and harmonious. This adventure had aligned us all and brought us closer together. I felt fantastic walking out of that hospital on New Year's Day.

I still had the ulcerative colitis to deal with. I made the decision to cease all immune-suppressing medications. It was a no brainer for me; I couldn't risk putting my body through that trauma again.

I discussed my options with my doctor and he was super supportive. He reinforced that I would never cure myself, but that I could possibly manage it through diet and healthy living only, and he was comfortable with me giving this new plan a go.

I respectfully told him I would cure myself, with food and with healthy living. He admired my determination, and sent me on my way, with the promise that I would check back in for follow up tests in twelve months.

Three years on, and I have no signs of the disease. My doctors have officially given me the all clear. I am eating whatever I like. I am listening to my body, and when I feel like I need to take it easy on certain food, I will avoid it for a while. I am doing healings on myself regularly.

I am meditating and trying hard to find a good life balance between rest and exercise, work and play, giving and receiving. The ulcerative colitis has gone! The doctors are surprised, and they warn me that it may still return. But I know I have got this; I have my own health and happiness in my hands. I am the creator of my own miracles.

I am in charge of my own health and happiness, and it feels fantastic!

DAD'S RING MIRACLE

When dad passed away in 2013, mum put his wedding band on her finger and she vowed never to take it off. When dad was alive that ring never left his finger, and now it was mum's turn to wear it with pride. This was her way of dealing with the loss of her husband. She needed to have that little piece of him with her, so she could hold his memory close. It gave her comfort and strength.

Mum would spin the ring on her finger; it was a fraction looser than her other rings, so it moved easily but was never too loose to risk slipping off. The ring-spinning became a habit, and it was soon something mum did without even realising it was happening. It became a natural gesture. Mum worked at a local supermarket, and as she busily packed groceries for her customers, the spinning of dad's ring on her finger was par for the course of her working day.

Easter weekend, 2016. Mum was working a shift at the supermarket, and her now natural gesture of spinning dad's ring suddenly made her stop in alarm. The ring was not on her finger. Panic sets in as she looks down at her hands in shock. No ring. All the staff begin frantically searching for the missing ring – scouring the floor, rummaging through bags, inspecting the cash register. Still no ring. Mum's work colleague calls me on my mobile to tell me the news. She says that mum is too distraught to talk and doesn't know what to do.

I immediately get a message from Spirit:

The ring will find its way back home.

Later that day, I tell mum that I'm positive the ring will be found. At this stage of my spiritual journey, not many people know of my psychic abilities and mum definitely isn't one of them, so I am careful about how I word my messages to her. I reassure her as best I can. I tell her it will all work out, I just know it.

The days and weeks go by. I keep getting the same message from Spirit, so I know the ring will be returned. I continue to reassure mum, and she wants to believe me, she truly does! But I think deep down she may have already been feeling like it was a lost cause.

Wanting to put the power of social media to good use, I created a public post the day the ring went missing, asking the public for help. This post was shared over one thousand times. And that's not including copy posts on local business and group pages, which were shared countless times also. So much love and support and well wishes were pouring in for mum. Hundreds of people were being tagged, in the hope of a regular shopper of that supermarket finding the ring.

Not for one second, did I ever think that the ring would be forever lost. I was holding out for a miracle.

On the third of June 2016, two short months after dad's ring went missing, I received a call from another of mum's work colleagues. She tells me mum is too upset to talk. She tells me a lady has just called the supermarket, saying she thinks she has a ring belonging to someone who works there. She left a phone number for someone to call her back, but mum was too nervous and scared to make the phone call. I take the lady's number and promise to call mum back straight away.

I dial the number I have just been given, anxiously waiting for someone to pick up. A lovely lady answers the phone. I explained the story of mum's lost ring. The lady tells me she has found a ring in the bottom of one of her old shopping bags. She tells me there is a date inscribed on the inside of the ring and proceeds to read the date to me – mum and dad's wedding day. We have found dad's ring! Just over two months ago dad's ring had gone missing, and it was now about to be returned to us.

Funnily enough, the lady doesn't have any connections with social media, so she never saw all the desperate pleas for help that were plastered all over the online community. She just happened to be cleaning out her cupboard one day and came across a pile of neatly folded shopping bags which were no longer being used.

She then did something she was not accustomed to doing; something she had no logical reason for doing. She felt the need to check all these folded bags to make sure they were empty before she tossed them away. She couldn't explain why she was overcome with this urge to check the bags thoroughly before disposing of them. They were folded and flat and she had never checked old bags like this in the past, before tossing them. I knew exactly why. Nice work, Universe!

My mum was reunited with her husband's wedding ring. There were tears of joy and amazement at this incredible stroke of good luck. The chances of that ring finding its way back to mum were not high. A supermarket has hundreds, possibly thousands, of customers coming through the doors every single day. Some are locals, and many are visitors and tourists.

The Universe works in mysterious ways, but it works. I never doubted that spirit message I received. I feel certain that going public, and in turn bringing thousands of people's attention to the ring, contributed to its safe return. All this attention flooded the situation with positive energy from everyone's kind thoughts, help and well-wishes. And we all know how powerful positive energy is!

MIRACLES OF ALL SHAPES AND SIZES

When I do healings for others, I am often asking the Universe to provide them with a miracle. And often, the Universe obliges. It must be for the person's highest good and for their greatest joy, for the Universe to provide these miracles. I have personally witnessed so many beautiful and amazing things happen to people, who come to me for healings and for spiritual guidance.

I have witnessed an alcoholic of forty years stop drinking. I have witnessed a well-travelled eleven-year-old child go from suffering through excruciating in-flight head and ear pain her entire life, to enjoying her flights pain-free. I have communicated with Spirit Guides who revealed the location of a lady's lost cat who had been missing for seven days; the cat was safe and sound and was reunited with its owner. I have witnessed a lady go from six years of broken sleep, to sleeping soundly all through the night. I have witnessed a man whose life support was about to be turned off miraculously regain consciousness, after receiving some energy healing at the request of his distraught family. All the above was achieved through trust and faith, and with the support of healing and spiritual guidance to the person involved.

I have witnessed many people suffering from chronic illness recover and achieve good health. I have witnessed many people suffering from depression and anxiety achieve happiness – some travel a slow journey of recovery, while others bounce back fast.

I have witnessed a lady's dangerously high blood pressure quickly drop to normal levels after only two energy healing and meditation sessions with me. The stories that have been shared with me, and those I have personally witnessed, of miraculous healing and incredible, almost unbelievable, strokes of good luck are endless.

We also need to pay homage to the smaller, often unnoticed, miracles. Let's take a moment to reflect on some everyday occurrences that, if you think about it, are miracles. Your lungs' ability to breathe, your heart's ability to pump blood, the miracle of conception, the miracle of new life in all forms – plants, humans, animals.

Miracles do happen all the time. All you need to do, is stay hopeful and believe.

14

MAKING A DIFFERENCE

'One tiny act of love creates a ripple effect.'

We all have the power to make a difference. You can make a difference to your own life, you can make a difference to your loved ones' lives, you can make a difference to humanity, and to our planet. It all starts with you.

You can lead by example; others will see you transform into a better, happier version of yourself and they will want to do it too. The best way to teach someone, is to live the lesson yourself. Be living proof that everything you are passionate about works for you. You don't need to force your views on others. You don't need to insist that everyone believes what you believe, or that everyone practices what you practice.

They will come to you when they are ready. They will become curious and want to know more. And when they do, you can use everything you have learned to help guide them to becoming a better and happier version of themselves. Sometimes, unsolicited help and advice works. But most of the time, advice works best when the receiver is ready.

The most effective way I know of, to make a difference and to teach others, is to live an authentic life. And to share my stories and lessons. This book is a way for me to share my life lessons on spirituality and enlightenment and healing and happiness, and those who are ready and eager to learn will read this book and soak up all the knowledge available to them. I use social media a lot to share my stories and to spread the love. Again, those who are ready to learn will follow my social media pages and those who aren't ready will scroll on by.

I believe that everything happens for a reason: people come and go from our lives, events take place, experiences are lived. We learn, we teach, we love, we connect, we thrive. And through this intricate journey of life, we are all constantly making a difference. Small actions, big actions, and everything in between. It all makes a difference. Spreading love as far as you can, is making a difference. Being your authentic, organic self is making a difference.

There are so many people I admire: famous celebrities and public figures, clients of mine whose lives are being transformed and enriched every day, my family and friends, and other healers and light workers. There are so many people making a difference to their own lives and to the lives of others. These are everyday people, and they are spreading the love. They are working hard at discovering their true, inner-self. So many people are making a difference, and many of them don't even realise it.

Speed bumps in life are lessons – they either slow us down, or they change our path. They get our attention, and for good reason. Go gently through the speed bumps, and you will eventually come out the other side as a better version of yourself.

Others will see that you are a survivor, that you are a warrior. Your life lessons can teach not only you, but others who are ready to learn too. So go forward with love in your heart and make a difference. It starts with you.

I used to feel extremely overwhelmed by the thought of making a difference in the big scheme of things. I used to watch the news and feel completely powerless. All the suffering and destruction and darkness in our world was sometimes too much for me to stand. I wanted desperately to fix it; to fix everyone and everything.

The sadness I felt for other people's suffering, all over the world, was debilitating. I just felt so *sad* all the time. Sad for the children who succumbed to violence and abuse. Sad for the mothers and fathers who were burying their children. Sad for animals who were suffering. Sad for humanity, because I felt like there was so much tragedy in the world and there wasn't a thing I could do about it. Oh, how wrong I was!

After spending months and months lost in a state of despair, I turned to meditation to try and pull me from the darkness I was being consumed by. It took me a few attempts, but at last, during a meditation, I could finally hear my Spirit Guides talking to me. I heard their whispers of guidance and encouragement. Their words came to me via thoughts in my head, that I knew weren't my own – it was not my voice I was hearing. I had no control over these soulful words that flowed through me, I just had to breathe, relax and pay attention to what my Guides were saying.

Here is what they said to me:

It all starts, with you and yours.

Along with these words, a general feeling of relief and hope washed over me. I felt as though I had been relieved of the burden of 'saving the world'. I knew where my focus had to be – on myself and my family. I knew that if I made a difference in my own life, it would somehow be making a difference to humanity. I didn't know how that was possible, but I knew I didn't need to worry about the *how*.

Those words and feelings I experienced during that meditation changed my perspective. It took my attention away from things I can't possibly control, to things I can control. It was this profound contact with my Spirit Guides that motivated me to keep filling up my own happiness cup, and keep sharing it with the world.

I still see and hear of terrible, heart-wrenching things happening all over the world, and it still affects me deeply. But I am no longer feeling helpless and this has made all the difference. I am confident that going about my day, spreading love and happiness as I go, is enough. I trust there are millions of other people doing the same thing – some intentionally, some unintentionally. I am confident that by working on my own happiness and wellbeing, and that of my family's, I am doing enough. And this is what you can do, too.

If you see or hear of something tragic going on in the world or in your community that affects you so deeply, and you can offer help in some way, then please do! I'm not suggesting you wipe your hands of all responsibilities, just of those you can't physically control. You can't let the world's problems consume you, nor can you ignore them.

You'll still hear of bad or sad things happening in the news, and when you do, go out of your way to smile and greet every person who walks past you in the supermarket, or every person you pass when you're out walking. This is enough. But if you have the time, money and energy to contribute more – like running a local fundraiser, or even getting on a plane and going to a struggling city or town to help the locals – do it! But only do these things, if it is within your means to do so.

You have a voice, so speak your truth often and with conviction. Make a stand by writing a letter, making a phone call, starting taboo conversations – even if it means you will go against the general flow of society. But again, only do these things if you have the strength and energy to contribute. You and yours must come first.

It is within my means to offer free healings to those in need and this is something I do regularly. I have a gift I can use to help others and they don't need to be in my vicinity to benefit, so this is one of the ways that I contribute more.

Let the bad stuff motivate you to do more good. You can't control the wars and the destruction in other parts of our world, but you can control how much love you send out to everyone around you – near and far.

We are all drops in the ocean of love. One tiny act of love creates a ripple effect; this love ripples throughout the Universe, reaching everyone and everything. Multiply that one tiny act of love by hundreds, or thousands, or even millions, and a tidal wave of love is created, washing over us all. It floods humankind and it floods our planet, saturating everything it touches with love, and leaving joy in its wake.

You are that one tiny act of love. Believe that everything you do has a flow-on effect. And believe there are millions of others who are also doing their one tiny act of love. We are all energy; we are all connected. Consciously add your love to the tidal wave to help it gain momentum and power, because this tidal wave is impacting on every single one of us.

PART III

SELF-CARE:

YOUR TURN

Now you have some good background information on soul energy and you are feeling inspired to work towards achieving true happiness within yourself. Let's now work through the how. How are you going to achieve this? The only way is by practicing self-care. I have talked at length about self-love, and now you are going to learn how to care for yourself on a deeper, more intimate and sustainable level.

How to actively show kindness to your own body and soul. How to nurture your body and your soul energy and hopefully, one day, be able to communicate with both. I will discuss different ways of practicing self-care including meditation, energy healing, nutrition and fitness of the mind and body, lifestyle choices, seeking spiritual guidance, and other spiritual practices. There are many other ways to practice self-care that aren't discussed in this book, so don't limit yourself to just these suggestions. Have fun exploring!

This section of the book is intended as an introduction to spiritual self-care. I am confident you will find at least one suggestion that resonates. The aim here is to inspire you to put more effort into the most important person in your life; YOU!

15

MEDITATION

'Once the mind is still,
your soul will shine through.'

By now, most people know about meditation. But do most people practice meditation? Probably not. Yes, many people meditate daily, but there are far more who don't. Which is such a shame because it's probably one of the most effective ways to single-handedly nurture yourself.

There are experienced professionals who specialise in facilitating meditations in towns and cities all over the world. But it's important to note that you don't have to spend money to be able to meditate. There are free apps for your mobile phone or device. There are thousands of free guided meditations, covering a multitude of different topics on a variety of video-sharing websites. A quick online search of 'guided meditation videos' is a great place to start. There are local groups who gather regularly to meditate, for a small donation or for free – you could likely contact your local Yoga or Wellness centre or perhaps even your local gym, for more information.

As the benefits of meditation are becoming widely recognised, schools are jumping on board and are integrating daily meditation into their lesson plans. The results? I asked several local teachers who have personally used meditation in the classroom, and they were quick to sing its praises. They all reported happier, more focused children. Many of these teachers reported less class disruptions and increased learning capacities in students who practice daily meditation. As a side note: if your child's school doesn't already do this, consider approaching the school's principal to explore it as an option. The kids, other parents and teachers will thank you for it!

Let's look at some of the benefits of meditation: stress-reduction, lowered blood pressure, reduced anxiety, improved immunity, healing of the body, improved memory, healing of the soul, deeper sleep, finding inner peace, improved focus, pain reduction, the list goes on and on. I could list many more benefits, but I am sure these select few have got your attention. These are benefits that either I have experienced in my own personal meditation practice, or that have been reported to me from clients attending my meditation classes.

There are many variations to meditation. Yoga – everyone knows about yoga! And yes, it's a form of meditation. I encourage you to do your research, find a meditation style that appeals to you, and give it a go.

BREATHING MEDITATION

If all else fails, do a breathing meditation. You can do it for one minute or thirty minutes, or however long you desire. The length of the meditation doesn't matter. What matters, is that the meditation is deep and restful. A five-minute meditation that is deep and constant is far more beneficial than a thirty-minute, sporadic and inconsistent meditation. We can all spare five minutes a day. Do it right before bed at night, or first thing in the morning when you wake. What a way to start your day!

Do you have children? Get them involved! Family meditations are a wonderful, healthy way to connect with each other and of course, everyone in the family can then receive the benefits. Do your own internet search of 'family meditations' or 'meditations for children' and you will be pleasantly surprised at the vast selection.

Back to the breathing meditation – if you have never done one before, follow these very easy instructions:

- *Find a quiet place* where you can sit or lay down, relax and close your eyes.

- *Play some soothing music* or sit there in blissful silence – your choice.

- *Start to slow your breathing* until it is controlled and deliberate. Do not rush yourself.

- *Inhale,* until you can't inhale any longer – challenge yourself to suck in that oxygen.

- *Hold your breath* for as long as it feels comfortable.

- *Exhale,* until you can't exhale any longer – again, challenge yourself to push out all that carbon dioxide. Push it out of your body until you don't have a single breath left inside you. Then exhale a little bit more.

- *Now inhale again,* this time breathing deep into your belly. Breathe in. Further, further…

- *Hold.*

- *Exhale.* Breathe out. Further, further…

- *Repeat* as many times as you feel the need, for as long as you need.

Your attention always stays with your breath. Your mind is thinking of nothing but your breathing. Breathing is your only focus. If you find your mind wandering, make the conscious effort to return your attention to your breath.

As you continue to practise this breathing meditation, you may find you can extend the time and last longer and longer with each session. Persistence and practice!

An even simpler alternative is to follow previous steps 1 through to 2. Then:

- *Rest both hands* on your abdomen.

- *Let your breathing flow* in and out of your body effortlessly.

- *Bring your attention to your hands* rising and falling with each breath in and each breath out.

- *Stay here* with your attention on your hands, as long as you need.

How did you go? Did you find it a bit tricky? Or was it effortless? Practice makes permanent! This meditation quietens your mind, allowing it to switch off. Not many minds have that luxury in this fast-paced life we all lead. Once the mind is still, your soul will shine through. And when that happens, you may experience things like flashes of colour or images, thoughts may pop into your head that aren't yours, your body may start to tingle and feel lighter.

Or, a nothingness may settle over you, comforting and healing you. This is all your body and mind connecting with and responding to the energetic elements of the meditation experience.

Don't be afraid. Keep breathing deeply and enjoy the experience. This intentional breathing meditation saturates your body with precious oxygen and because of the deep, deliberate breathing, your diaphragm is filling up and this in turn is massaging and stimulating the neighbouring internal organs. It is detoxifying, it releases stress and anxiety and it promotes sleep. If there is only one self-care practice that you want to master, make it this one.

If the thought of meditation still doesn't appeal to you, perhaps the following suggestions will resonate. Have you ever considered that listening to your favourite music, whether that be pop, rock, classical, hip hop or any other genre, is a form of meditation? If there is something you love to do that makes you feel all the good stuff and it feels ritualistic, even if it's pottering in the garden or tinkering in the shed, it's a variation on meditation.

My husband is a mechanic and has been his entire adult life. His passion is cars. For as long as I have known him, one of his favourite things to do is disappear to the shed for a couple of hours.

I asked him one day what he does in there and he told me he turns his music up loud, then immerses himself in some form of mechanical or fabrication activity while sipping on a beer or two.

I've since watched him work; he loses himself and all sense of reality when he does this. He is creating, being in the moment, working with his hands, feeling the vibrations and sounds of the music. The music he plays could be anything from heavy metal to country music. Once he has closed himself in his shed, I can usually expect to see him surface again in at least a couple of hours, sometimes longer.

Early on, I used to be a little annoyed by his need to retreat to his shed. You know, the usual complaints such as: there are jobs that need doing around the home, he should be spending that time with me or with the kids, or his music is too loud.

Now, I get it. This is his meditation.

My daughter also has her own form of meditation. She is a dancer and has taught herself everything she needs to know about makeup. For her this is an art, a real passion.

I've stood in her bedroom doorway and watched on as she's carefully opened her makeup bags and methodically laid each item out on the floor in front of her. She, too, has music playing while she meditates; her favourite music is rap. As the lyrical words pour from the speaker, she ceremoniously begins the process of applying her makeup.

Her father and I feel she is still too young to wear a full face of makeup out and about, but this doesn't stop her from doing what she loves. She isn't putting on makeup to mask herself. She is doing it because she enjoys the process. It is therapeutic and it is creative.

She, too, can spend anywhere from an hour onwards just sitting on the floor, in front of the mirror, with her makeup splayed around her, using a combination of intuition and creativity and some really impressive skill to apply her makeup. Then she'll spend the rest of the day pottering around, enjoying her masterpiece.

So you see, meditation can be done in many ways. Sometimes, all it takes is a change in perspective to see that things you do every day are a form of meditation. And once you have made this realisation, and you give yourself permission to lose yourself in the moment, you will notice a remarkable change in how these activities make you feel.

Meditation is a game-changer; it heals your body, your mind and your soul all at the same time.

16

SPIRITUAL HEALERS APLENTY

'The opportunities to explore and learn more about spiritual healing are endless.'

Are you feeling tired, stressed, emotional, or all of the above? Do you have aches and pains that come and go, and no one can seem to find the cause? Having trouble sleeping? Trouble with relationships? Trouble with your health? Then the odds of you needing a spiritual healing are pretty darn high.

Energy healing is like taking meditation to the next level. Spiritual healing rebalances and fine tunes your soul energy, so that it flows beautifully and leaves you feeling energized, lighter and happier.

There are many different types of spiritual healers. If you are feeling overwhelmed by choice, try not to overthink it because they all have similar benefits. Trust your intuition and what you are feeling drawn to. Healing practitioners all have their own unique style, which is a good thing! Two healers may be trained in the same modality, but they each put their own unique spin on it.

They, too, are using their intuition.

We are very spoilt for choice. Reiki, Shamanic healing, Aboriginal healing and crystal healing are all examples of the wide range of healing modalities available to you, which we will discuss in much more detail throughout this chapter.

There are always new energy healing modalities being created by healers who are discovering their own unique method and then teaching others their craft. They all have their merits and benefits.

All healers, no matter what label they give to their craft, are connecting with the same energy. The energy of the Universe. The only difference is how they connect, what they witness and how they work with this energy.

THE ROLE OF THE HEALER

When I make reference to a healer, I am using this term for the sole purpose of being relatable and identifiable to the wider public. I refer to myself as a healer.

Really, I am a facilitator and a conduit of the universal life force energy. It is not me doing the healing – I am holding space and conjuring the energy. It then flows through me and into the person on my healing table.

So you see, technically I am not a healer. I am a witness. However for ease of understanding, this is the title I have chosen to use. There are many people who have very strong views of people adopting the title *Healer*. They believe it is a misrepresentation of what we do, of what our role is, and that it discredits the practice.

To the wider public, I have chosen to refer to myself as a healer – after very careful consideration. It feels right and the title *Facilitator* just doesn't have the same ring to it. I make it clear every time I perform a healing for someone exactly how the healing works, and what my role in the process is. My clients, in my care,

are under no false impressions.

Let's now discuss your role in the healing process, because it's your role that takes centre stage. It is your role to actively participate in and be present for the duration of the healing. This is your healing journey. So, in a sense, *you* are the healer. You are your own healer – we are all our own healers, each responsible for our own spiritual well-being.

No two healings that I perform are ever the same for me or for the receiver. Release all expectations and be prepared for the unexpected. Healers share the same responsibilities and expectations, regardless of the modality we are using to connect with the energy. We must always work from a place of love, not ego, so the healing can be the best possible experience for all involved. A healing will always then be for the highest good of the receiver; you.

REIKI

Most of what I am sharing with you here, is from my own experience and training as a Usui Reiki Master-Teacher. Reiki is the healing modality that introduced me to the universal life force energy. In other cultures, other teachings and other communities, different techniques are used to tune into this same universal energy, but these techniques will vary greatly and will all have very different names and interpretations. I believe it is all essentially one and the same; the healer is connecting with the energy and channelling it into the receiver.

So, as you read the following paragraphs on Reiki, please keep in mind that much of this information is relative to all forms of energy healing. What sets Reiki apart from other channelled energy healings, is the Reiki symbols. These are a set of specific Japanese symbols used to generate and activate the energy.

The traditional form of Reiki, Usui Reiki, was founded in the early twentieth century by a Japanese monk, Mikao Usui. *Rei* translates into *soul* or *spirit*, and *Ki* translates into *vital energy*. Reiki is an ancient Japanese healing modality that allows the practitioner to channel universal life force energy into the receiver and this powerful energy then flows through the receiver's body, mind and soul, assisting them to heal and repair. This flow of energy comes through the practitioner's hands.

Some practitioners work strictly with the original teachings of Mikao Usui. Other practitioners, through working with their intuition, have adapted the original teachings to suit their own individual healing styles. All qualified Reiki practitioners, despite the method they currently use in their practice, have received the appropriate training they need to provide a healing experience for others. The most important thing for you to remember, during your search of a qualified Reiki practitioner, is trust. If you feel comfortable in their presence, you have found the healer for you. It is normal to feel nervous during your first Reiki healing, because you really don't know what to expect. But deep down under the nerves, there should be feelings of trust for your practitioner.

Every living being is connected to the universal life force energy and we are all born into this humanly realm with a connection to the Universe that is deep, strong and pure. Unfortunately, many of us, as the years progress and we are exposed to the everyday stresses and pressures of life on this Earth, experience an ebb in our connection to the Divine. A Reiki Practitioner, through their attunement ceremony, re-establishes that original, pure connection to the universal energy so they can then harness this energy and channel it into the receiver.

During a Reiki healing, you are fully clothed and usually laying down, or sometimes comfortably seated. If you and your Reiki healer are not able to be physically together, the Reiki energy can be sent to you long-distance, if your practitioner is trained appropriately.

Reiki is suitable and safe for everyone young and old including children, pregnant women, and even animals. Reiki works well in conjunction with Western Medicine; it is intended to complement, not clash with, orthodox medicine. Reiki can do no harm, ever. It can help with a whole range of symptoms and ailments including mental health, physical illnesses, and emotional health. Reiki, like all energy healing, gets to the root cause of issues. It goes in deep, to the energetic and spiritual level, which is where I have found most illnesses and ailments to originate from.

Reiki was the modality that crossed my path and opened me up to the incredible world of energy healing. When I discovered Reiki in March 2015, it changed my life. Very soon after that, I witnessed the power of Reiki changing other people's lives, as I began to provide energy healings for the wider community. I could share with you countless stories of how the healings I have been involved in have helped other people from a whole range of physical and psychological illnesses, chronic injuries, emotional trauma, fears and phobias, but I will instead share with you one particular story that has touched my heart.

Eric is a young man who is one of the most loving, attentive, sensitive, intelligent and cheeky people I have ever had the pleasure of meeting. Eric's healing journey with Reiki started when I crossed paths with his beautiful mother at a spiritual wellbeing expo, and from the moment I laid eyes on him, I knew he was special. Eric was born with a condition that the doctors describe as being very similar to cerebral palsy. Eric has battled with his health his entire life including chronic pain, sleeplessness and anxiety. Eric's open-minded parents, who are his full-time carers, turned to energy healing to see if it could offer him any relief.

Eric may not be able to communicate verbally, but his soul energy and body language speaks volumes. From the very first Reiki session, I could sense the sharp intelligence of his mind and his sensitivity to energy around him. I could sense the energy of his internal organs, his digestive system and other internal systems, none of which were functioning well.

Since Eric has been receiving Reiki healings on a regular basis, his parents have noticed significant improvements. The often debilitating, chronic constipation has significantly lessened. The frequent, chronic pain episodes that would grip Eric for hours in violent body rocking and loud moaning are now few and far between. Eric's parents say that his anxiety has drastically reduced, particularly when he is out in public. They say, overall, he is happier now than he has been in years. In fact, Eric is now often heard chuckling to himself or laughing out loud – his parents are thrilled to see him so joyful!

I have also taught Eric how to harness the healing power of Reiki using various techniques, to help him deal with physical, emotional and energetic issues that arise. His mother has since witnessed him using these techniques on several occasions, with her gentle encouragement when she has noticed him become uncomfortable or in pain, with significant and often instant improvements.

It was a regular occurrence for Eric to need the first half of his summer holidays to recover to a settled and happy state, so he could then enjoy the last half of his holidays at home with his family. The care group activities would begin again for the new year, and within days of being around other people and in other places, the unsettling symptoms would return. His mother says this cycle no longer exists; Eric no longer needs weeks to recover from being out and about in public with his care group every day, around other people and their energy. Reiki has helped strengthen and protect his energy so he can now go about his daily life, without being consumed by the energies around him.

Reiki is helping Eric. And it is helping so many other people all around the world from all walks of life, with all kinds of ailments and issues. You don't need a religious faith and you certainly don't need any experience or knowledge in energy healing to benefit from Reiki. As I say to all my clients: keep an open mind, let go of all expectations, and let the energy work with your mind, body and soul so you can heal. Find yourself a healer you trust and enjoy the journey!

ABORIGINAL HEALING

The Aboriginal people are Indigenous Australians who, much like most other indigenous cultures around the world, have their own spiritual healing practices. These practices are based around their beliefs of what is commonly referred to as the *Dreamtime*. Dreamtime is the English title (a generalised translation) of the traditional Aboriginal philosophies and way of life. Whilst the entire belief system of an indigenous culture cannot be expressed or justified using just one mere word, for ease of understanding, Dreamtime is the phrase I will use throughout this section, with the utmost respect to Aboriginal people.

The Aboriginal people believe everything in the natural world was created by their Spirit Creators – the Ancestral Beings – and that many of these Ancestors eternally exist in the land, the animals, the stars and planets, in the wind and rain, in all of nature. The Ancestors and the Dreamtime are not a thing of the past, they are everything everywhere, past present and future.

The various aboriginal mobs throughout Australia have a strong connection to Dreamtime. They connect to Dreamtime through their everyday life, through ceremony, through their laws, and through the sharing of Dreamtime stories.

These stories are about the creation of all life, and of connection to land and to spirit, that have been handed down from generation to generation. The Dreamtime is the foundation for the Aboriginal way of life, the rules by which they live, and the way they interact with the natural environment. It is an all-encompassing concept that integrates ancestry with daily reality.

Danny Gardner is a young Tasmanian aboriginal man who lives and breathes the tradition of his people. Danny is a proud descendant of the Trawlwoolway people of Larapuna country, Lutruwita. *Larapuna country* is the Bay of Fires region, on the north east coast of *Lutruwita* (Tasmania). He has a powerful connection to his people, to his culture and to *country* (the land), and I am privileged to have been invited to spend some time with him, to learn more about the Aboriginal people's healing practices and beliefs.

Like all true healers, much of Danny's knowledge, skills and gifts comes from an innate inner knowing. Despite having spent a great deal of time learning from local and interstate Aboriginal healers and elders, Danny says many of the things he knows can't be attributed to any teachings he has received in this lifetime. It is in his blood, and in his spirit. Danny offers traditional Aboriginal healings to those who reach out to him; people who often have already exhausted all other means of finding happiness and good health through Western Medicine.

It is no coincidence that Danny recently sought the help of my mechanic husband to do some maintenance on his vehicle, at the exact time I was creating this section in the book on Aboriginal healing. It is important to me that I include the healing traditions and practices of the Australian Aboriginal people in this book, because I have a profound respect for and admiration of their culture. I am, after all, residing on their sacred and beloved *country*.

I spent hours making phone calls and sending emails to various people and groups, and doing extensive online research, yet I couldn't find the information I was looking for.

I was becoming increasingly frustrated and feeling a little

disheartened. I was beginning to wonder – do I need to respectfully leave the Aboriginal traditions alone? Should their healing practices remain secret, only to be shared within their own community and not with the general population? I wasn't sure how to proceed.

So I sent a little prayer out to the Universe. *Please, if this needs to be shared, send someone my way who can help me learn more about Aboriginal healing.* Then guess who turned up? Danny! He, out of the blue, after doing a quick online search for local mechanics, contacted my husband. While they were working on Danny's vehicle, the two men got to chatting. One thing led to another, and my family and I now have a connection with someone who is going to enrich our lives in so many ways. Danny and I have crossed paths for a reason, and I am feeling very blessed to now share with you an insight into traditional Aboriginal healing, through the eyes and spirit of Danny.

At the heart of Aboriginal healing, is a connection to country. This concept of *on country healing* that Danny refers to implies that we can all heal, if we reconnect with the land and with nature.

ABORIGINAL ON COUNTRY HEALING

Danny's advice for a quick pick-me-up or to release any tension or stress, is to go for a slow walk through nature. Every couple of minutes, stop walking and very slowly and deliberately turn around, to take in the whole 360-degree view. Absorb all your surroundings through all your senses and your body, mind and soul will reset.

You will feel the tension leave your body and you will feel lighter, as *country* heals you.

This very intentional stroll through nature can be an extremely powerful experience for everyone. This *on country* healing is something you can do, that costs you nothing, yet will leave you feeling energized and refreshed. All you need is an open mind, good intentions, and some time to meander through nature.

One sunny Saturday afternoon, Danny guided my children and I through an Aboriginal *on country* healing through ceremony. Before we all set off into the bush together, a huge male wedge-tailed eagle was spotted flying high in the sky, right above us. He circled for quite some time, before he parted ways.

This majestic bird welcoming us was no coincidence – Danny's spirit animal is the eagle; it is the soul of his grandfather who watches over him and his young son. To see the knowing smiles on the faces of Danny and his son, as they acknowledged the presence of the eagle and of their ancestors was priceless.

We were then greeted by a large family of magpies and another family of butcher birds, who all came in close to say hello. These birds almost appeared to have been summoned, on cue, like our own personal welcoming party. There was a special kind of magic in the air that day! The land had acknowledged our presence and was giving us its blessing to proceed.

Danny walked us through the bush, with his son leading the way – who was happily playing his clapsticks; a traditional Aboriginal musical percussion instrument made from wood. Danny hand-carved his clapsticks from the wood of a wattle tree and, when struck together, they made a beautiful sound. The shrill and crystal-clear pitch of the sticks echoed through the bush around us. We were on our way.

Danny foraged for live branches of a species of Australian native peppermint gum to use in the healing. As he silently and respectfully asked for permission from the grand old tree, he gently removed a handful of new, young growth. He parted ways with the tree, with a sincere *thank you*.

Everything Danny did that afternoon, the walking, the foraging, the setting up of the space, all in preparation of the healing, was having an impact on him. Every step he took was changing him. Every time he collected some more dried grass to keep the little fire burning, he changed. The entire experience from beginning to end was a powerful and sacred act for him, and it showed.

We reached the spot where the first stage of the healing was to take place, and we helped him gather dried grass, bark and twigs to make a small fire. As he ceremoniously assembled and then lit the fire, I could already feel the energy in the space around us shifting.

Danny and his son opened the healing with a traditional *Welcome to Country* ritual, letting the Aboriginal Spirit Ancestors know of our presence, and asking for their blessing to be there. He gave each of us a piece of the peppermint tree foliage, and instructed us to brush the branch all over our body – in doing this, we were passing all the old, bad *spirit* from ourselves to the branch.

He told us to think about all the things we want to release, as we were brushing ourselves. Any problems or worries, any anger or sadness, was all passed on to the tree branches.

We were then offered some ochre paste – a simple blend of pure, naturally sourced ochre and water – to paint our bodies in any way we felt comfortable doing. This is to establish a deep connection to the land. We smeared the red, gritty paste on our hands, arms and faces and Danny and his son even rubbed it through their hair. He then demonstrated how to use the young branches of the peppermint tree to cleanse our spirit.

One by one, we took turns in placing our tree branches into the fire. As the smoke rose from the green leaves, we smudged ourselves by fanning the smoke over our bodies, until every single green leaf had been burned. The smoke carried all the negative energy away, into the wind and the elements. We were cleansed.

By this stage we were all feeling quite different to when we first arrived. The collective feedback from the cleansing ranged from feeling light and floaty, to feeling deeply emotional and on the verge of tears without knowing why, to feeling empty, and one person couldn't even articulate what they were feeling because it was so powerful. Danny extinguished the little fire, and then led us up another track in the bush, to the top of a small hill.

On top of the hill was a large stone circle, and Danny explained that as we stepped inside the circle, we were protected. This circle is where Danny and his friends come together to dance; it is their sacred space. He said up there, the sun can recharge our spirit.

So we all ambled around the circle, casually chatting and exchanging stories, as the sun refuelled our souls. Up there, the wind was quite strong but it didn't feel like any ordinary wind to me. Usually, a strong wind will agitate me to the point that I need to seek shelter, and fast. This wind felt energizing. It felt as if there was something unseen, being carried in the wind towards us, and it too was recharging our spirit. The energy up there on that hill was powerful! And we all felt it, especially the children.

By the time we had walked back to the carpark, everyone was different. I could see a brilliant sparkle in the eyes of both Danny and his son. I felt exceptionally calm and relaxed, despite having done quite a bit of walking. Both my children said they felt different and, to me, they had changed dramatically, although I wasn't quite able to pinpoint *how* they had changed. There was a definite change in every single one of us.

We had walked *on country*, connected with the wildlife, cleansed our spirit with fire, and then refuelled under the sun. All in a day's work, for an Aboriginal healer. But Danny doesn't consider this his work, he considers this his duty. It's his role to take care of the land and in return, the land will take care of him.

The relationship between the Aboriginal people and their country is a joy to witness. Their connection to their Spirit Ancestors is humbling, and their ability to heal their own people and others who are open to it, is honourable.

Aboriginal healers are not easy to come by because as a whole, they are very private people. So if you do one day happen to cross paths with an Aboriginal healer, like I was lucky enough to do, consider it a little gift from the Universe. I highly recommend you add this experience to your energy healing wish-list, because it is a rare experience that can not only heal you through spirit, it can heal you through nature.

At the very least, getting outdoors and intentionally walking through bushland is a healing experience in itself. Combine this with the spiritual elements of Ancestral Beings and Spirit Animals, and you have yourself one very potent recipe for happiness and good health.

SHAMANIC HEALING

Shamanic healing is an ancient spiritual practice where the Shaman healer connects with nature and enters the spiritual world to access wisdom and healing for their client. The Shaman is able to enter an altered state of consciousness so they can communicate with spirits to receive guidance and healing. This is known as a shamanic journey, where their brain enters a theta state. The brain waves slow down and the mind enters a state somewhere between awake and asleep, similar to hypnosis.

Once the brain is in this relaxed state, they are then able to connect fully with their soul, as it journeys through the spirit world while holding intention and purpose to achieve what they have set out to do. Many everyday people take themselves on shamanic journeying meditations, to take them to this spiritual realm so they can work on their own journey of self-discovery and enlightenment.

However if it is deep, spiritual healing you are after, you should seek out the services of a responsible and reputable Shaman. The

Shaman may use an array of Shamanic healing techniques and rituals, using tools such as drums and crystals alongside the shamanic journey to give you an experience that you won't forget!

A Shamanic healing is ideal if you are feeling stuck in your life. If you have lost or can't find your purpose. If you are searching for clarity and direction. Perhaps you feel like there is something missing from your life, but you aren't quite sure what that is. It is also ideal for past trauma healing. A Shaman will get to the energetic roots of your current life position, seeking spiritual guidance and facilitating deep energetic releases. The Shaman is there to guide you on your soul journey, offering support and guidance along the way.

A Shamanic healing or journey is such a unique and earthly experience. Shamans are very connected to the Earth and to nature; they are healers of the land. Traditional Shamans and Shamanic practices have been found in all corners of the globe, although within their own culture and language they may hold a different title.

The exact origin of the word *Shaman* is unknown and there is little historical evidence to support the precise translation of this word. Many anthropologists believe it originates from Siberian Russia in northern Asia, to loosely mean '*to know*' where other researchers and experts believe it translates as '*one who is excited, moved, raised*' or, '*a social functionary who, with the help of guardian spirits, attains ecstasy in order to create a rapport with the supernatural world on behalf of his group members.*'[1]

A Shaman is a revered member of the community and is held in very high regard. They are the gifted member of their group who enters the spirit world and returns with healing, messages and guidance to benefit others.

---

1 An Encyclopaedia of Shamanism Volume 1, Christina Pratt, 2007

Historians have discovered that Shamanism, in the traditional sense, has been around for tens of thousands of years and, thankfully, these ancient Shamanic teachings and gifts are being passed down through the generations so that we, as a modern-day society, can still connect with and benefit from Shamanic practices.

I sought the help of a local modern Shaman to help me establish better balance and connection between my physical and energetic self, and to connect with other aspects of my soul-self that were yet to be discovered.

The journey took place in her yurt on a beautiful bush property in southern Tasmania. A yurt is a round tent-like structure, traditionally used as a dwelling by nomadic groups in Central Asia. The lining of my Shaman's yurt was decorated with gifts of the Earth such as wood, crystals and bird feathers, and a little pot belly wood fire sat at the heart of the yurt.

We sat facing each other and as she picked up her drum, I could see she was already beginning the transition to the spirit world. She closed her eyes, began a slow and rhythmic beating of her drum, and then she was gone. She was now walking through the spirit world, alongside me and my Spirit Guides. She talked me through our journey; her words were poetic and descriptive and the tone of her voice blending with the beat of her drum was mesmerising. I too, closed my eyes.

We journeyed through a landscape dotted with shadows and cliffs with our Animal Guides beside us – a black jaguar and a sabre-tooth tiger. She explained how details within the landscape represented energetic boundaries that needed to be crossed.

Throughout the journey, she called on help from other spiritual beings and entities and they joined with us to help us cross the boundaries. She spoke of a masculine aspect of me, of my soul, who also met with us to walk us through the journey.

He and I walked together through the earthy landscape while our two energies balanced one another; masculine boldness and pride, blending with feminine humility and tenderness.

Her imagery was stunning. She described my soul energy opening and changing as it met the golden light of the sun. We descended into lush, green valleys and gullies abundant with new life, connecting me with new and abundant soul energy.

I then became one with the masculine aspect of my soul's past. The sound of the river babbling and bubbling past us in our spirit world created a fusion of two liquid souls – our two souls became one entity of water. As one, we connect and communicate. As our energies meld together, we become one energy.

The disturbances within my physical body are corrected. The porous nature of my body allows me to absorb great amounts of wisdom and knowledge. She now sees me in my human form within the journey, and I have changed. I now have a gentle sheen of light overlaying my body; my skin, my hair, even the fibres of my clothes are now interlaced with a higher energy. The integration is complete.

My Shaman delivered many messages from Spirit, all very relevant and comforting. These messages have inspired me. The journey has energetically shifted things inside me that were previously blocking me from moving forward with my body, my mind and my soul in harmony. This journey has also helped to energetically align me with my purpose as a healer; it has fine-tuned the way I connect with and work with others when helping them on their own spiritual journeys.

I am not hung up on expectations of what the future holds, as a result of my Shamanic healing. The journey, the experience itself, was a valuable and truly memorable encounter. Whatever happens as a result of this is a bonus and a blessing. I felt a shift within myself during the experience. I also felt deeply relaxed, centred and at peace with myself and with everything and everyone around me.

I now continue to feel my soul coming into greater alignment with my purpose and with my body. Everything I had originally hoped for, as a result of the Shamanic journey, is now happening.

I believe the important thing when embarking on an experience such as a Shamanic healing or any other deeply spiritual energy healing, is to try and release all expectations. Sometimes, when we get in our own way, we will miss the subtle little shifts and blessings that cross our path.

So, for example, if you are holding on to an expectation of achieving perfect health after a healing, instead of feeling grateful for the changes that do occur, you will feel disappointed. You will miss the other little miracles that are happening in and around you.

Surrender to the experience and to the outcome. Set an intention, and then let go and enjoy the ride. Your ability to trust is a huge part of achieving your spiritual, health and happiness goals. So trust as best you can, then acknowledge the gift you are receiving and *enjoy* the experience!

CRYSTAL HEALING

Crystals and gemstones are extraordinary spiritual healers! I could talk about crystals all day. Who doesn't love a spectacular little cluster of clear quartz? Or a perfectly purple amethyst geode? How about an elegant blue sapphire ring?

For one, crystals and gemstones are stunning to look at. They are extremely popular additions to home décor and jewellery collections. And the incredible Earth energy they all hold and radiate, is second to none; just hold one, you'll see!

There have been occasions where I have walked into a crystal store and was moved to tears from the overwhelming energy pulsing through the store. The energy in a crystal store affected me so deeply once that I had to leave the store to compose myself!

If you have never tried it before, the next time you come across a crystal in a shop, hold it in your hands, or touch it if it's a big one, and close your eyes. Feel its vibrations in the palm of your hand, as it connects with your own soul energy.

Can't peel your eyes away from a particular crystal? Are you feeling drawn to it? That crystal is calling you! It is connecting with your soul energy and sending it a message. Don't resist it, go to the crystal and allow yourself to feel it, physically and energetically.

Does it arouse emotions deep within you? Allow yourself to feel those emotions, then thank them and let them go. You are experiencing an energetic release here, with some help from your crystal.

There are healers who harness and use crystal energy to heal their clients of a wide range of physical, emotional and spiritual conditions. Different crystals hold different energy, and a crystal healer has an expansive knowledge of the different crystal types and knows how to use these different Earth energies to heal their clients.

Crystals were mined by the Ancient Egyptians. They held crystals in high esteem, *'not just because of their visual effect in a particular application, but also for the symbolic or magical significance of their colour.'* [2]

The Ancient Greeks also revered crystals and gemstones, placing a very high value on them. Here's a fun fact: The word amethyst comes from the Greek word *amethystos* meaning, *not drunken*. According to Greek mythology, amethyst had the power to keep people from getting drunk! Which is why wine goblets from that period were often carved from amethyst.

Have I inspired you to dig out your old crystal collection? Or to go and buy a little beauty that you feel attracted to?

---

2 James Harrell, University of Toledo, OH, Environmental Sciences, UCLA Encyclopaedia of Egyptology 2012

Crystals are a great addition to your life, because they come in all different shapes, colours and sizes. And they vary in price from just a few dollars to thousands of dollars. So you can be as frugal or as extravagant as you choose.

CLEANSE YOUR CRYSTALS

There is a little bit of maintenance that goes with being a crystal owner; they do need cleansing from time to time, and there are a few simple ways to do this, depending on the type of crystal:

- *Lay them out in the sun* and let the energy from the sun's rays cleanse them.

- *A popular method is to lay them out during a full moon*, allowing the energy from the moon to cleanse them.

- *Rinse them under running water.* Be careful with this one, because some crystals and gemstones don't like being wet so be sure to check first whether this is suitable for your crystal.

- *Use visualisation techniques* to cleanse your crystals. Thoughts are energy, therefore we can use our thoughts, through visualisation, to work with energy. An example: hold your crystal in your hand and imagine you are drawing all the old energy out of the crystal and into your hand. Then imagine your hand is releasing that old energy and it will go back to Mother Earth, where it will be recycled and renewed.

I recommend cleansing any new crystals that you acquire, so their energy is fresh and clear, ready to assist you on your healing journey.

Crystals are such a fun addition to your life; they can bring you joy and lots of special healing vibes, so if you don't already own a crystal, I highly recommend getting out there and finding one that appeals to you.

BE YOUR OWN HEALER

All other energy modalities and techniques aside, you *can* heal yourself simply by laying your hands on your body and holding the intention that *you are healing yourself*. You don't need to spend any money to be able to harness and use the universal life force energy that we have already discussed in detail.

Yes, studying and practicing a specific healing modality will help and heal you. And yes, working with another healer will help and heal you. But ultimately, all you need is determination and persistence. I know of many people who have never been formally trained in any energy techniques, yet they can feel the energy flowing through their own body, as they intentionally and intuitively place their hands on themselves. Learning a specific method or technique will enhance this gift we are all born with, but it is not essential.

Do you want to explore your gift and what you are capable of, as the healer of your own body, mind and soul? Try this:

> **SELF-HEALING**
>
> Bring your hands to the prayer position at your chest (your heart space).
>
> Close your eyes.

Say in your mind, or aloud, your intention of channelling universal energy for the purpose of healing yourself for your highest good.

Allow your breathing to settle, allow your body to relax.

Breathe. Relax.

Breathe. Relax.

Notice your hands, how do they feel? Do they feel heavy, or perhaps they feel light as a feather? Do you feel your hands being overcome by any tingling or pulsing, heat or cold sensations? Or maybe your hands feel neutral. Despite how your hands feel, know that the universal life force energy is being harnessed by you. You know that the flow of life is coming in through your crown chakra at the top of your head, and is coming out through your hands. You know that the energy is accumulating, as the flow gains strength and momentum in between your hands like an almost-tangible sponge of lightness.

Breathe. Relax.

Place your now-highly-charged hands somewhere on your body. You might like to start at your head and methodically work your way down your body. You may like to start at your feet, working upwards.

You may feel the overwhelming urge to lay your hands on a specific part of your body. Your hands may begin to tingle furiously, as the energy is released into your body, or they may feel numb or heavy. You are the witness. You are observing the feelings in your hands, and in your body, as the energy flows through you.

Breathe. Relax.

Hold your hands on your body for as long as you need. It may be a few minutes, or longer. You may need to move your hands to different positions on your body, as the healing progresses. Know that you are more familiar with your body than anyone else on this Earth. You know what your body needs – what it wants. You maintain an unwavering trust in your ability to provide yourself with health, happiness and inner peace.

As the flow subsides, your healing is now coming to a close. For now. You resolve to revisit this sacred space of personal healing often and always.

You know that the more you persist, the stronger your healings will become. You know that you are doing this for your own highest good and greatest joy.

You hold no expectations; you simply surrender to the flow and bear witness to the magic. That is your role to play: breathe, relax, witness.

During the healing your mind may wander, this is okay. You may feel discomfort, this is okay. You may feel emotional, this is okay.

Let go.

Surrender to the flow that is embracing you, move through the emotions and the aches and pains. Gently steer your mind back to your breath, back to the flow.

You may like to keep a journal of your healing adventures. As you continue with your healings, you *will* experience great things. And not just physically, spiritually and emotionally.

You will also notice subtle changes in other aspects of your life; relationships, encounters, everyday experiences will change. This is all part of the healing process – change. Knowing this, embrace the changes and get busy living. Integrate your healing practice into your daily routine, whether you can afford ten minutes or an hour, a little is better than none at all.

THE HEALING POWER OF WORDS

I would now like to invite you, if you feel inclined, to participate in a healing through the written word. As you slowly and meaningfully read the script on the following page, know that the healing light and love will flow through the words and into you.

As I am typing these words, I can feel the energy in my hands begin to stir. There is an aching sensation radiating up my forearms, in readiness to release the healing words on to this page.

I can feel my crown chakra expanding with the influx of light and love and I smile, recognising all of this as I have done many times before, as the beginning of the wondrous craft of healing. This healing is yours to use as often as you need. Cherish it, as it cherishes you.

LOVE THYSELF

I am a heavenly soul on Earth, walking my path.

I am loved.

I am supported.

I welcome the lessons and the change.

I embrace happiness and inner peace.

I am one with eternity.

I am the Divine.

And the Divine is me.

Balance.

Love.

Truth.

Real.

Stunning.

Joy.

I release all that is no longer serving me, with love.

Heal.

The multitude of healers discussed in this chapter are just a small selection of what is out there available to everyone. Here are some other healing modalities I am currently aware of, that I feel are worth mentioning: Forensic Healing, Akashic Healing, Pranic Healing, Quantum Healing, and Theta Healing. As always, do your research first. Go with what feels right for you. Ask for recommendations from family, friends, or the local community. You'll be amazed at what is available to you! There is a healer out there waiting to meet you.

Spiritual healing is a vast and wondrous medicine. So vast, in fact, that I don't think we, as humans, will ever be able to fully comprehend it. But this is why I love it so much! The opportunities to explore and learn more about spiritual healing are endless. And the opportunities to learn more about yourself and what you are capable of, through connecting with this incredible energy, are also endless.

Spiritual healing has the potential to take you to other realms or realities. The only reality that most people acknowledge is this physical realm, but we can go beyond this reality, through our awareness of energy. Spiritual healing has the potential to take you inside yourself, to show you glimpses of past lives and of past trauma so you can heal, to show you the energy in various shapes and forms, to feel the energy coursing through your body either in subtle tingles or intense waves.

Everyone can learn how to connect with and work with energy. And you don't need any prior experience or knowledge in either the medical, scientific or spiritual fields either. I have witnessed hundreds of people, who had no prior knowledge of or experience with spirituality or with energy, transform their lives for the better.

All you need is an open mind and be ready to actively participate in your healing journey. It is such a widely available, yet unique way to empower yourself and reclaim your health and happiness.

I feel very blessed to have discovered this incredible, life-changing arena of spirituality and energy medicine. It captivates and intrigues me. It is certainly not for everyone, and I respect that. We all have our own path to walk and if spiritual healing still doesn't resonate with you at all right now, that's okay!

Maybe one day, when it is the right time for you, you will become curious about spiritual healing. When that time comes, pull this book back out and give yourself a refresher.

If that time is now, embrace it and keep an open mind. If things confuse you or alarm you, then leave them alone. You are not yet ready for that. If, as you are progressing on your spiritual journey, things feel like they are happening too fast and it's overwhelming you, know that you have the power to slow it down. How? With your intention. Just send a little message out to the Universe, or to your Spirit Guides, to please slow down.

But if it feels right and you are getting fulfilment and enjoyment from it, then keep going. I guess those same principles apply to everything in our lives. If it resonates, go with it. If it doesn't, let it go. Just because something works wonders for your best friend or work colleague, doesn't necessarily mean it will work wonders for you.

I learned that lesson through many years of trial and error. A lot of what I tried didn't work for me, but it has worked and is still working for many other people. We need to learn to trust our own judgement, which is why it is crucial to learn to listen to your own intuition, because it never lies.

This is why I want to encompass as many self-care tips as possible in this book; to give as many people as possible a variety of options, so the chances of you discovering a self-care tip that resonates is very high. The more self-care you give yourself, the more you love yourself and the stronger your intuition becomes.

17

ENERGY MEDICINE

'Every day, someone new discovers
energy medicine and it changes their life.'

If the thought of a deep, spiritual experience is a little unsettling for you right now, don't despair! Because there are other ways to heal your soul energy and to bring more happiness and health into your life. We will now discuss some of the other energy therapies and techniques you can try which are all nice, gentle buffers to the deeper topics and experiences discussed in the previous chapter. Then, when you've had a chance to test the waters of energy medicine in this context, you may feel ready for a more ethereal spiritual experience.

All the information in this chapter complements the spiritual healings beautifully – so if you are ready to embrace it all, there's no reason why you can't experience them all, in whichever order you prefer.

TAPPING

Also known as EFT (Emotional Freedom Technique), tapping is a technique involving the stimulation of specific meridian endpoints, combined with repetitive spoken word. Meridians are the energetic pathways that flow through the body, according to Traditional Chinese Medicine.

According to tapping therapists, tapping encourages the body, mind and soul to release negative energy in the form of tensions, memories, emotions and physical injuries.

While the meridians in the body are being stimulated through the tapping, you would first voice the negative emotions being experienced, followed by voicing some positive affirmations specific to the issue being dealt with. Say, for example, you have low confidence and this is something you would like to address. Whilst gently tapping the specific meridian endpoints, you would start by saying some things like:

'I have low confidence,'

'I have low self-esteem and I don't know why,'

'I feel sad and frustrated by this,'

Once you have worked through this negative mindset and acknowledged your emotions and how you feel and how it is affecting you, thereby releasing the negative energy, you continue the same tapping sequence and move on to the positive affirmations:

'I am a confident person,'

'I can easily make eye contact with people,'

'I feel free,'

'I feel light,'

'My confidence empowers me,'

You get the idea! These positive affirmations, from an energetic viewpoint, are projecting a whole lot of positive energy to the issue you need help with. These positive affirmations are also helping to create a healthier mindset, through repetitive behaviour. These messages are delivered to the body, mind and soul through both the spoken word and through the tapping of the meridians.

There are tapping practitioners who specialise in this form of energy healing, or you can learn to do it yourself. There are benefits to having a practitioner perform the tapping healing; they are using their skills and experience, combined with their own intuition, to accurately target the areas in your body or your life that need attention. Sometimes, when you are in the throes of something big, it can be a good idea to reach out for help from someone who can be impartial and who isn't emotionally attached to your issue; a tapping therapist would be ideal.

Tapping is extremely effective for healing emotional trauma. In fact, a quick online search will show that many reputable psychologists and councillors are now promoting the integration of this healing technique as a treatment component of their client sessions.

The act of tapping can also be a very grounding experience, helping to keep you connected to your body while you work through emotional trauma with your therapist. It helps to keep you present.

It is also used to provide what psychologists refer to as *sensory input* which, in everyday language, is a way to re-program the neural circuits in your brain, through the repetitive sense of touch. In other words, tapping can rewire the brain to respond in healthy ways.

Tapping is reportedly a great way to relieve stress! Many people tap their meridian endpoints to diffuse a build-up of stress in their body and mind, and the results are often instant.

On the following pages, you will find a tapping exercise you can try the next time you feel stressed.

First, I'll walk you through the tapping sequence.

Note: It doesn't matter how many fingers you use, and you want to apply gentle pressure; don't hurt yourself! The exact spot isn't important; the approximate area is totally okay. It doesn't matter which side of the body, or which hand you use; you can do both sides, or just pick one.

Okay, here we go with the tapping sequence:

TAPPING SEQUENCE

First position: outside edge of hand (between little finger and wrist)

Second position: inside edge of eyebrow (top of eye socket)

Third position: outside edge of eyebrow (outside edge of eye socket, near temple)

Fourth position: bony ridge beneath the eye (bottom edge of eye socket)

Fifth position: between nose and top lip

Sixth position: crease between lip and chin

Seventh position: collar bone (can use whole hand, or all fingers, for seventh, eighth and ninth positions)

Eighth position: side of ribcage (about a hand-width below armpit)

Ninth position: top of head

This is a full circuit of the tapping sequence.

Now that you have the hang of the tapping sequence, it's time to add the element of repetitive spoken word. As you work through the above tapping sequence repeatedly, you verbalise your thoughts:

SPOKEN WORD

Begin with a verbal intention of unconditional self-love, while tapping on position one – your hand:

'Even though I am stressed, I love and accept myself.' Repeat this a couple of times, while still tapping on position one, if you feel inclined.

RELEASING THE NEGATIVE

Then work through the remainder of the tapping sequence, from position two through to position nine, while you verbalise your truth – your inner thoughts. This is your opportunity to vent:

'I feel stressed,'

'I feel angry,'

'I don't know why I feel this way,'

'I'm so sick of feeling this way,'

'I feel stressed,'

'I am tired,'

'I can't do this anymore,'

These are just suggestions; whatever words come out of your mouth, as you tap through the first few rounds of the sequence, are right for you. You are venting. *You are releasing.* You can continuously work through this cycle, from position two to position nine, repeating this cycle once, twice, three times, or more, while saying whatever statements come to mind. Keep going with the releasing of your fears and frustrations, until you feel you can move to the next stage of the healing.

REINFORCING THE POSITIVE

Next, you are working through the same tapping sequence, from position two through to position nine, while making some positive statements around your stress, such as:

'I am doing this,'

'I am strong and I am getting through this,'

'This is easy,'

'This is safe,'

'I am okay,'

'I am calm,'

'I am happy,'

And so on. Again, these are just suggestions. Try saying whatever positive thoughts spring to mind. Repeat this positive cycle as many times as you need.

Once you have worked through your intention, worked through the negative, then worked through the positive, you need to close your eyes and take a big, deep breath in, then exhale. Re-centre yourself. Let it go. You should then feel so much better than when you first started! You can repeat this whole sequence as many times as you like – some people only need one full round, where others will work through the tapping sequence for an hour or so.

Some people notice immediate improvements, while others need to persist with it for a few days, but with practise, your mind, body and soul should begin to respond faster and faster with every tapping experience.

Use this technique as often as you need; let this free tool help you work through the stresses and negative moments in your life. And not only that, it can help you achieve a better night's sleep, a better relationship with food, with loved ones, with yourself. It can help you release anything you are internalizing, so you can be calmer and happier and enjoy a more healthful life.

ACUPUNCTURE

Acupuncture is a Traditional Chinese Medicine (TCM) healing technique, where fine therapeutic needles are inserted into the skin, targeting different points along the meridians – the energetic channels within the body.

I had a chat with Dr Sarah George, a registered and qualified Acupuncturist, so she could give me some more insight into this modality. Sarah says historians date acupuncture back to around 200 BCE and it became popular in the West, following Richard Nixon's visit to China in the 1970s where he observed a surgical procedure undertaken only with acupuncture anaesthesia. Today, practitioners have the benefit of understanding the classical theories and techniques from the documented historical texts, as well as being trained in the latest developments in Western Biological Science. Modern day acupuncture is therefore a unique fusion of Traditional Chinese Medicine with Western Medicine.

Sarah says, traditionally in TCM terms, acupuncture rectifies the flow of qi through the meridians and through the flow of blood in the body. *Qi* is the TCM term for the body's life force or soul energy. This means if the qi is stagnant, acupuncture helps it flow. If the qi is rising too much, acupuncture can lower it and on the other hand, if the qi is sinking, it can be raised through acupuncture. If the qi is flowing in the wrong direction (known as rebellious qi), which can present as a cough or vomiting, acupuncture can help to harmonise. There may also be a deficiency of qi or blood, which can also be addressed. Sarah says, sometimes external forces such as Cold, Heat, Wind or Damp can penetrate the channels and cause stagnation (which is often associated with pain). The emotions also affect qi, such as – anger makes qi rise and worry knots qi, like a knot in the stomach.

During a treatment of acupuncture, you can expect to go through a thorough and holistic assessment of your main complaint as well as your general health, because it is seen that the systems of the body all influence each other. Practitioners may also consider blood test results, imaging or other Western diagnostic methods. This, and much more, is assessed by the practitioner which then leads to a Chinese Medicine Diagnosis.

You are then positioned comfortably on a treatment table, where the acupuncture will take place with the aim of remedying the diagnosis. Sarah says many first-time clients are afraid of the needles hurting, but she finds most people don't experience any pain. Registered Acupuncturists are well trained and are required to abide by specific guidelines put in place, for the safety of the patient.

Acupuncture is typically a very relaxing treatment, with many patients falling asleep due to the deep relaxation experienced. Many people report sensations in their bodies during a treatment, such as warmth or a releasing feeling.

Sarah says Chinese Medicine has a strong commitment to nurturing and preserving life, known as Yang Sheng. With this in mind, your practitioner may prescribe changes to diet, exercise, sleep, or the way you manage your mental or emotional health.

Depending on what you are seeking treatment for and the severity of it, you may need anywhere from one single treatment to around three months of treatments. Some people seek the help of an Acupuncturist to manage a degenerative condition and in this case, treatment would be ongoing, as necessary.

One of the most profound experiences Sarah has had with acupuncture, was when she was a teenager. She had developed an ear infection in both ears and was in tremendous pain. She was unable to eat or talk and she had already been through three courses of antibiotics.

After a single acupuncture session, her pain had reduced significantly and by the next day, her ears were unblocked and the pain was gone. She has also experienced almost instantaneous results from acupuncture for blocked sinuses.

Acupuncture is popular in sports therapy and sports rehabilitation, and in pain management including chronic pain. Acupuncture is likely more widely accepted by society and by Western Medicine than other healing modalities, because of the physiological science behind it and because of the long, documented history of use and a growing body of research supporting the therapy.

While you wouldn't treat yourself with acupuncture, there are other techniques you can learn which have similar effects to the needles, such as *acupressure.*

An acupressure technique I was taught a few years ago, has served me and my family well for a variety of aches and pains. Whenever someone in my family experiences a muscle spasm or sudden muscle pain, I apply pressure using my middle finger and move it around the area until we have located the exact spot of the pain. We know when I have hit the spot that needs acupressure, because the pain will intensify significantly.

Once this trigger point is found, I apply firm pressure to this point for anywhere from a few seconds, to a minute or two. I release the pressure, and then apply it again. Repeating this, until the pain eases.

I don't apply too much pressure to cause extreme pain or discomfort; the pain should be bearable. This isn't necessarily a relaxing experience for the receiver! But it's efficient; it gets the job done quickly.

The next time you are feeling run down or moody, try using acupressure to help release your tensions.

Follow along with this simple acupressure exercise, and see how easy it is to do something nurturing and healing for yourself:

ACUPRESSURE EXERCISE

Using all fingers, prod and poke all over your feet – top and bottom, sides, toes, in between toes, all over, until you find a specific spot that feels more painful or noticeable than the rest. You will know it when you find it!

Once you have identified this point (which, if you then did some research, would discover it's most likely a meridian endpoint), apply firm pressure with your finger or thumb, until the pain or discomfort subsides.

Then give yourself a good foot rub, to complete your diy acupressure session!

If you aren't game to give acupuncture a go or have a fear of needles, consider acupressure. Although it may not be as powerful as acupuncture, it is less intrusive and still highly effective. However I do hope that after reading this section on acupuncture, you are feeling more informed and therefore more confident to give it a go.

I have a fear of needles and I survived acupuncture! It didn't hurt at all – I felt a little discomfort in one spot, but as I relaxed more, the discomfort disappeared.

Acupuncture is a very powerful means of healing. Although acupuncture, through the insertion of the needles, appears to be more intrusive than other energy healing modalities, it is a very safe, gentle therapy that can be beneficial for a whole range of physical, mental and energetic ailments. Again, as with all therapies, you must find a reputable, experienced professional whom you trust, then let them guide you to wellness using acupuncture and Traditional Chinese Medicine.

GROUNDING OR EARTHING

Another energy medicine technique that is important to discuss, is the act of grounding or earthing yourself. If you are unfamiliar with this, it is the act of physically and energetically connecting yourself to the Earth's energy.

In doing this, you are balancing your own soul energy. In doing this, you are plugging into the Earth's energy and recharging; you are strengthening your energy. And you have many options to choose from.

A technique I use a lot because it is accessible and free, is the act of putting my bare skin in contact with the ground. Bare feet in the grass or sand works wonders. Or you can lay yourself down on the bare earth, for a little rest with nature. Bare skin is the most effective and because water is a conductor of energy, if the grass or sand or dirt or other earth surface you are laying on is wet, it will heighten the grounding experience.

You can also purchase grounding devices. Earthing sheets or mats and even shoes are now widely available. Ever since my husband and I have had an earthing sheet on our bed, his snoring has dramatically reduced. And this wasn't even why I bought the sheet! I bought it to help give our overall health a boost – with some niggly little aches and pains in mind. The aches and pains have reduced significantly and to top it off, we are both sleeping much more deeply and soundly. Earthing is pretty amazing!

If your home has copper pipes and metal bath fittings, you can ground yourself in the bath. The metal pipes are a conductor of the Earth energy, so the energy then travels up the pipes, and into your bath full of warm water.

Some people like to use visualisation techniques if they need grounding in a hurry:

EARTHING VISUALISATION EXERCISE

Close your eyes and imagine yourself standing on a beach; the warm white sand beneath your bare feet.

Now imagine that the Earth's energy is radiating through you; it's coming up from the sand, into your toes and feet, up your legs, past your hips and over your stomach, flooding your chest cavity and overflowing down your arms and up through your neck and filling your head.

Remember, thoughts are energy, so any visualisation that you do is sending powerful energetic healing to the recipient which in this case, is you. Grounding yourself can achieve so many things: it can heal your energy, it can strengthen your energy, it can cleanse your energy and it can protect your energy.

You may like to set an intention as you are grounding yourself to achieve any of the above. Or perhaps you may prefer to ground yourself simply with the intention of receiving whatever it is your energy needs at that moment, for your highest good.

CLEANSE YOUR ENERGY

Many people don't realise how much external, negative energy we all pick up as we go about our day. Have you ever walked through a crowd of people and come out the other side feeling completely drained? Or have you had a person unload all their worries on to you, and you come away feeling awful and they walk away feeling fabulous?

You are being bombarded by negative energy around you, and sometimes you absorb this negativity, without meaning to, leaving you feeling less than great – especially if this negative energy accumulates over time. You can either go to an energy healer to get a cleanse and rebalance, or you can do it yourself.

I always teach my clients how to cleanse and clear their own energy, as a way of maintaining the clarity of their soul energy after a healing with me. Part of my job is to show my clients how empowering it is to take charge of their own energetic well-being.

My favourite way of cleansing my own soul energy is in the shower:

SHOWER CLEANSE EXERCISE

While in the shower, close your eyes and feel the water running over your body and imagine the water washing away all old, negative, unwanted energy and rinsing it down the drain, where it will be returned to Earth to be recycled and renewed.

And that's it! Again, visualisation is key. Bad energy will be gone, and you will step out of the shower feeling light and fabulous.

Children are very susceptible to picking up other energies around them, particularly at crowded schools and day care facilities.

You can help cleanse your child's energy by doing this same practice; get them in the shower and use the same visualisation process for them. Ask your child to participate in the imagery as well, because kids have extraordinary imaginations, so take advantage of this and get them joining in on the fun.

STRENGTHEN YOUR ENERGY

It is important to keep your soul energy strong, and there are so many ways of achieving this. But don't feel overwhelmed, because we have pretty much already covered them all.

Grounding, chakra healing, tapping, meditation, practicing self-love, enhancing your intuition – this all strengthens your soul energy. Any time you practice a spiritual or energetic exercise, you are exercising your *soul energy muscle*, which gives your soul energy strength. Any type of healing work you do for yourself, or that you receive from other therapists or healers, is strengthening your soul energy.

The stronger your energy becomes, the happier you will be. You will feel stable, assured, centred, balanced and joyful – you will feel incredible!

The more effort you put into yourself, the stronger you will become. And not just stronger spiritually; you will become stronger in mind and body as well.

PROTECT YOUR ENERGY

Now that your soul energy is grounded, clear and strong, there are some techniques you can learn to protect your soul energy. By protecting your soul energy, you are shielding yourself from the constant flow of negative energy around you.

I use the following technique to protect myself when I know there will be lots of people around me, such as a concert, party, or any other big social gathering. Before you or your family head out next time, try this visualisation technique out:

> **BUBBLE MACHINE EXERCISE**
>
> Close your eyes and imagine there is a giant bubble-making machine in front of you.
>
> Imagine this machine is blowing out a huge bubble, especially for you. The bubble is whatever colour you want it to be, and any shape you want it to be. Know that you can get creative with any of your visualisation techniques that you use!
>
> Now imagine that beautiful big, safe bubble, full of positive and nurturing energy, closing in on you.
>
> It gets closer and closer and it eventually encompasses you. You are now inside that bubble and you are safe.
>
> All the lovely energy inside that bubble is now protecting you.

I know of a teacher who used this technique for a child in her class who was a highly sensitive, emotional little soul. She reported that the child now seems happier, more settled and is engaging with the class more. So if you are a teacher, give this a go!

If you have your own children, put them all in their safe little bubbles before they head out for the day. Better yet, teach them how to do it for themselves.

Another of my favourite protection techniques, is to imagine that my own soul energy (or my aura) is being pushed out in all directions as fast and hard as I need it to. The reason I love this technique so much is because it works in two ways. It a) protects you from other negative energies around you and, b) gives everyone and everything around you a super potent blast of love and light.

Protecting your energy will dramatically reduce the negative energy you absorb as you go about your day, however some will still sneak through. You will still need to cleanse and strengthen your energy even if you are protecting yourself, you just won't need to do it as often.

If you can combine all three elements of energetic self-care – cleanse, strengthen and protect – you will feel like a whole new you!

HOLISTIC MEDICINE

Every day, someone new discovers energy medicine and it changes their life. I truly believe all these energy healing modalities and other reputable and responsible therapies will soon weave their way into mainstream Western Medicine.

I don't believe one style of healing or medicine is better than the other. All of it combined – western science-based medicine and spiritual, energy, and holistic practices – can work together for the betterment of everyone.

There are already news articles gaining a lot of attention about hospitals around the world offering energy healing to their patients. I personally have done countless energy healings on registered nurses, surgeons and other Western Medicine professionals who are now singing its praises.

I sold an item on an online marketplace not so long ago and the buyer, through making conversation, asked me what I do for a living. I told him I was a healer. He smiled and said he was a paediatrician who specialises in acute care for sick children in our local hospital. He is also a qualified Reiki Practitioner. He shared stories with me of using energy healing on his young patients and the incredible responses he has witnessed.

He is combining his paediatric expertise with his spiritual gift, to help sick children heal. But he is, for now, having to do it discreetly. He can't yet openly tell the hospital staff or many of his patients what he can offer them, so he does it quietly. His incredible gift is mostly going unnoticed by the wider community.

There are thousands of others out there just like this man, masking their true capacity for fear of being shamed or ridiculed for it. There are also other medical professionals who, although they may not endorse energy healing or spirituality, still respect it. My surgeon, who was treating me for ulcerative colitis, was one of these open-minded professionals.

'You go and do whatever you need to do to heal yourself,' he told me.

Energy medicine wasn't something he professionally supported, but at the same time, he was supportive of me and my decisions and that made all the difference. He didn't understand it, in fact I don't think he believed it would work at all, but he didn't once make me feel like I was foolish for believing in energy medicine or for being a spiritual person.

I was able to successfully use a combination of both medicines to heal myself. This holistic approach of blending spirituality with science was vital for my health and wellbeing. So don't be afraid to confide in the medical professionals you encounter on your healing journey and don't be afraid to start conversations about energy medicine.

As more people enquire about energy healing and other alternative therapies within our hospitals and health-care systems, there will be the birth of a Truly Holistic Medicine System. Modern day science and technology is saving lives. Ancient, traditional healing techniques and beliefs are also saving lives. One is not superior to the other. The more people talking about energy medicine, and not in a superior 'I-know-better-than-you' way, the more likely it will become a normal part of everyday conversation. The more this is woven into everyday conversations, the more wide-spread it will become – resulting in more people finding health and happiness.

18

NUTRITION AND FITNESS OF THE MIND AND BODY

'Thoughts are energy, so send as much positive energy into your food as you possibly can.'

There is tremendous focus on good nutrition right now. All you need to do is check out the trending news to see what I am referring to. As I write this book, there are numerous diets circulating that are a hot topic of conversations. People are avoiding gluten and dairy. Some avoid meat. Others are only eating raw food.

I am providing healings for clients every day, who have sought my help for their food allergies and intolerances, and the numbers are increasing. People are desperate to heal their bodies using food. I believe food is an important part of self-care, but it shouldn't be the only part of your self-care journey.

Many people are busting themselves trying to eat super-healthy food, doing all the right things (by other people's standards) by avoiding some foods and eating more of others. It is creating a lot of stress and anxiety for many people, as they desperately try to heal their bodies of many different diseases and ailments.

Autoimmune disease is a huge issue for many people right now. A professor at Harvard Medical School states that, *'Autoimmune diseases have become almost epidemic.'*[3]

People's bodies are seemingly attacking themselves from the inside out. Does this sound like a happy and healthy way to live your life? No way.

Nutrition is a passion of mine; I am certainly not an expert in this field, but I have been researching nutrition for over ten years. I know all about salicylates and amines and gluten and dairy and healthy fats and lacto-fermented foods and drinks. If you don't have a clue what I'm talking about, you don't really need to. My point is, what works for someone else may not work for you. Someone may come to you and say, 'Oh my goodness, I feel amazing now because I have stopped eating all dairy products! You need to give up dairy, it has been a life-changer for me!'

Or perhaps at a family get together, your aunty corners you. 'Salicylates are the reason I have been so unwell! You have to stop eating them immediately, you will feel so amazing if you do!' she says.

You race home and immediately research salicylates and become overwhelmed by all this new information that is being thrust at you.

These well-meaning people have just experienced a huge revelation and they want to share their success with as many people as they can because they want to help. Their intentions are good! But these conversations can have a huge negative impact on other people's lives. If it does work for the other person, that is fabulous! I, myself, stuck to a strict diet of no grains, dairy or potato for a little while and it was great. I have also gone just dairy free for an extended period. And I have eaten a low carb, high fat diet as well.

---

3 Jessica Lau, The Harvard Gazette, 2019

But I can't sustain any of them long term.

I tried to push myself through – telling myself that it was healthy and the best thing for my body, even though I was miserable because I felt chained to the kitchen and was spending all my money on food, and before I knew it, I had a borderline eating disorder.

I had become afraid of food. And it wasn't anyone else's fault! It was my own fault – I wasn't listening to my body or my intuition.

Every now and then, I will still go back to limiting certain foods for a little bit, if I feel like my body needs it. For example, sometimes I stop eating dairy products for a couple of weeks to give my body a break. But now I know when either my body has had enough or it needs a little more, and I change my nutrition to suit.

If a nutritional choice isn't working for you, it can leave you feeling disheartened and depressed. Believe me, I know.

THE FOOD DISASTERS

When my children were babies, I was on the edge of an eating disorder. I had been to see a naturopath who told me that under no circumstances should I eat any grains apart from rice. I was also told to cut most other foods out of my diet, until I could work out what the culprit causing my skin allergies and inflammation was. I took her advice too far.

I had become afraid to eat anything else, for fear of my skin allergies flaring up. Funnily enough, those same skin allergies were at an all-time raging high, even though I was following my therapist's instructions implicitly. My obsession with rice became out of control and before too long, plain cooked white rice was virtually all I was eating.

I lost so much weight to the point that, according to my worried mum, I looked gaunt, fragile and unwell. This was not a fun time and was not easy to recover from. My unhealthy obsession with food had me in its grips, and I was suffocating.

A few years later, my obsession with food reared its ugly head again. My husband and I attended a friend's wedding and it was such a great day! The reception that evening was at their home, which was about a ten-minute walk from my home. They served lots of decadent, delicious food and my wheels came off big time.

I had been eating nothing but white rice and other bland food for weeks prior to the wedding – again, trying to fix myself and too afraid to eat anything.

I decided I was going to live a little that night and eat the beautiful food that was on offer. They had a talented chef prepare their food especially, it was nutritious and wholesome home cooking. As soon as the food hit my lips, I knew I shouldn't be eating it. I knew my digestive system wasn't strong enough to handle this feast. But I ignored those feelings and ate, just like everyone else. I didn't want to be different. I didn't want anyone to know about my unhealthy relationship with food.

For the next five hours, wearing stiletto heels and a gorgeous full-length dress, I ran backwards and forwards from their home to my home so I could have the privacy of my own bathroom.

I had an extremely upset tummy, who was letting me know in no uncertain terms that I had made a terrible decision. I would run, in the dark by myself, back to my house – three blocks away. I would sit on the toilet for a while to relieve my poor tummy, then I would attempt to compose myself and run as fast as I could, in my evening wear, back to the party, hoping no one would notice I was missing.

I lost count of how many times I did this throughout the night. And I tried so hard to hide it from everyone, even my husband had no idea what I was going through. It was our friend's magical day and I didn't want to ruin it because of my terrible relationship with food.

That night was exhausting. My poor body was spent. By the end of the night, my feet were numb, my bottom was in excruciating pain from all the aggressive bowel movements, my tummy still ached and I felt really, really… really unwell. I also felt ashamed. I was so upset with myself.

If you feel like you have an unhealthy relationship with food and you can relate, even just a little bit, don't lose hope!

Perhaps you have just added another diet or eating plan to your long list of *diets that don't work for you*, yet it is working for thousands of other people. What is wrong with you?

I am here to tell you, absolutely nothing is wrong with you. Your body is unique; it has its own genetic makeup and DNA; think of this as being your own molecular fingerprint.

Your body also has its own cells and organisms and of course, your soul energy is yours alone – there are no carbon copies. So, it makes sense that a diet working for one person may not work for another. It makes sense that my friend Lucy can eat spinach with every meal and feel amazing, but this gives me an upset stomach.

We humans have a pretty good understanding now about body functions such as gut health. There are a vast array of scientific studies featuring gut health and gut flora that have taught us so much about how our bodies work, but there is so much more to it than science may ever know.

Judging by the hundreds of healings I have done over the past few years, and through listening to the bodies and souls of others communicating with me through these healings, and through my own personal research on nutrition and physical health, I have learned that our bodies are complex organisms on so many levels.

I have learned that we have billions of miniscule bacterial colonies living inside us and on us, and they play a crucial role in the overall health of our bodies and minds.

I have learned that depression and anxiety have been linked to poor gut health. I have learned of people who very strongly believe that conditions such as autism are linked to poor gut health. Eczema and dermatitis have also been linked. There are so many theories and ideas floating around right now about nutrition and how it affects our bodies, and it's because people honestly do want to help each other.

We all want to have happy, healthy bodies and we want to help others have happy, healthy bodies. But where do you draw the line? How are you meant to know what food agrees with you and what food doesn't?

INTUITION AND FOOD

Remember that little thing called intuition? That, right there, is how you are going to do it. Use your intuition! If someone tells you that you must cut out grains and dairy because it is the healthiest for your body, pause for a second and pay attention to how that statement makes you feel.

Does it resonate with you? If so, then give it a go! And if you are following all your flash new cookbooks and whipping up some incredible meals for yourself, and you eat something that upsets your stomach or makes you feel meh, listen to your body! It is telling you that it doesn't like or need that food right now. If following your books outlining your new eating plan causes you excess stress and anxiety, then have a break. Don't keep forcing yourself through things that don't feel right.

As a little side note here, sometimes the body can go into a state of detox as a result of improving your eating habits. Which unfortunately means that sometimes you could make a great food choice whilst listening to your intuition, and it results in you feeling anywhere from a little out-of-sorts to very unwell.

This may be a sign that your body is experiencing a detox; meaning your body's ability to rid itself of toxins has been kicked into overdrive. This is a good thing! However, as the toxins are released from your body, they may make you feel very ordinary. So again, it is important to not only listen to your body, but also to your intuition.

If you experience any detox-style symptoms after you have made an adjustment to your eating plan and you can't work out if what you are experiencing is because of a detox or because your body doesn't need that food, check in with your intuition. You can then work out whether to soldier on, or whether to make some further changes. Don't forget to refer to the handy intuitive tools and exercises discussed earlier in this book, if you need some extra help. Your pendulum and the Sway Test will both serve you well in this instance.

Usually, detox symptoms last anywhere from a few hours to a few days. In extreme cases, they can last weeks. I went sugar free a few years ago, and two days into my sugar free eating plan, the detox kicked in. I had chronic headaches, body tremors and extreme mood swings for a few days, then it all subsided and I felt probably the most amazing, physically and mentally, I have ever felt!

I now have some more insight I would like to share, regarding children. Throughout this book we have already discussed how intuitive children are. Children being intuitive with food is alive and well, but it is often mistaken for 'fussy eating'. Does your child love bananas one day, and then refuses to eat them the next? Does your child constantly refuse a healthy food that you keep offering them because you think it is good for them?

Maybe you have a fussy eater on your hands, or *maybe* you have a very intuitive child who knows what their body wants and needs nutritionally and energetically.

A couple of years ago, my daughter came down with a nasty virus and she was one very unwell little girl. I asked her what her body needed to support it while it fought the virus and recovered, and she instantly replied, 'Watermelon!'

She did nothing but rest on the couch, sip on water, and eat watermelon for two days, and she recovered faster than I have ever seen in the past. She literally ate no other food for those two days. She didn't need any medication or other intervention; she had what she needed to heal. Watermelon is still often her go-to remedy when she feels an illness coming on. Her illnesses are shorter-lived and are not as severe.

[It would be irresponsible of me if I didn't make mention here of the importance of seeking medical advice if and when it is needed. Please always consult your healthcare professional when it comes to any illness or issues with your little ones, if you have concerns for your child's health!]

Does your child always change his mind when it comes to food? I used to get very frustrated by my children's constant 'mind-changing' when it came to meal times. One day they loved spaghetti bolognaise and would demolish a big serving of it in a flash, and the following week or fortnight, they didn't want to eat it at all. Now, I take all their comments and feedback on board, so I can try and accommodate their needs and support them as they learn to become intuitive little humans.

Obviously, you can't be expected to prepare separate meals for each member of your family to accommodate everyone's nutritional and energetic needs at that time. But what you can do is get your children involved in the grocery shopping. Ask your son what fruit he really feels like this week – he will know. Ask your daughter which vegetable is her favourite right now – she won't hesitate to tell you. If they aren't sure, teach them the Sway Test!

Eventually, with practice, they will no longer need the Sway Test because they will have developed their *inner knowing*.

So keep this in mind the next time your child refuses food or complains that she is sick of it or doesn't want to eat it, because she may just be relaying to you those internal messages that her little soul is sending her growing body.

ENERGY AND FOOD

Are you going around and around in circles trying to figure out what specific food is causing your body so much turmoil? If you are at this point, you are probably so wound up over food in general that no matter what you eat, it is going to disagree with your body.

Why? Because food is stressing you out, big time! Not just any food, all food. And all those panicked, stressful thoughts you are thinking as you prepare and then eat the food are channelling lots of negative energy into the food, so this food isn't going to be good for you and it's not going to be any good for anyone else who eats it, either.

Do you scold yourself if you eat a chocolate bar? Do you hate yourself for eating that ice cream, or even that piece of fruit? These are more negative thoughts that are being channelled into your food. There is no shame or harm in stopping this nutritional rollercoaster you are on. Get off it, right now. Regroup. Remind yourself why you are doing this in the first place; to heal your body and be happy.

If it is causing you so much angst, it obviously isn't working. Remind yourself that food is healing and nourishing and tell yourself this, as you cook the food and as you eat it. Thoughts are energy, so send as much positive energy into your food as you possibly can.

Have you ever been gifted an old family recipe for a dish that just blows your mind with delight when you eat it, but when you follow the same recipe and use the same ingredients, it just doesn't taste the same? Does it now make sense why this happens? Because your great, great grandmother would have cooked with love in her heart. She would have poured all her soul into that dish, and that right there is why it tasted so damn good.

When you cook your next meal, think of this story and cook with love in your heart. Don't cook when you are upset or angry, because you and your family don't want those negative emotions floating around in the dinner.

I did an experiment on this recently. I cooked my whole family a roast lamb for dinner, like I always do every week or so. All I put on it was salt and pepper, like I always do. I cooked it at the same temperature, for the same time I always do.

However, as I was preparing the meat, I channelled as much love as I could muster. I gave a strong, silent *thank you* to the animal, who's meat we were about to consume. I thought of the love I have for my family, as I prepared the meat to go in the oven.

Dinner was served, and every single person at the table could not believe how delicious the meat tasted! They raved about it – and my family don't often rave over my roasts. They always like a roast, but never love it. On this particular night however, they absolutely adored it. I was feeling pretty chuffed with myself that night.

I tested the theory again with a few other dishes that aren't typically family favourites, and I had the same results. Positive thinking wins again!

Cook with love. Imagine being able to heal your children with food! Pour all your love you have for your children into the food you are preparing them and notice the difference. A mother's cooking used to connotate images of bliss, happiness and comfort. But most mothers today are so busy and stressed, so our meals tend to fall a bit short in the bliss department. It doesn't have to be like that. Get back to basics and please cook for you and your family with love.

Yes, people have allergies and intolerances and I know from first-hand experience that these are difficult to deal with. But if you keep these few tips in mind, you will make your life and your relationship with food so much easier:

- Cook with love.

- Eat with love.

- Eat slowly and enjoy your meal.

- If someone else's food advice doesn't resonate with you, leave it.

- Use your intuition. If it feels right, do it. If not, leave it.

- Understand that food is fuel not just for your body, but your soul too.

- Be gentle on yourself, this is a journey and you are learning as you go.

- And most importantly do not beat yourself up for enjoying 'bad' food in moderation.

HERBS, BEAUTIFUL HERBS

Do you want to go next level? Combine your awesome instincts with the healing power of herbs. Herbs and herbal medicine are a true passion of mine. If you can introduce some extra herbs to your diet it will transform your health and wellbeing. Herbs generally don't get enough credit for what they are capable of.

Herbs have been used by humans for millennia for treating common ailments, illnesses, injuries, mental health, physical stamina and performance, among so many other things. You're just going to have to take my word on this one. From my own experience ingesting herbs and using them during meditations and healings, and from spirit messages I receive for other people that involve the use of herbs in a variety of ways, I have learned that herbs are everything.

You may be surprised to learn that common herbs found in most home gardens such as parsley, rosemary and thyme just to name a few, have *incredible* healing qualities. And the bonus is, they taste so good! What many people consider weeds such as dandelion and milk thistle, contain a synergistic cocktail of essential vitamins and minerals for good health, just as leafy green vegetables do.

Become better-acquainted with herbs, you won't regret it. They are cheap (often free), easily accessible, easy to grow, they make beautiful additions to every garden, porch, or kitchen, and they are crazy good for you! What more could you possibly need?

Intuitively select your favourites and sprinkle them generously, fresh or dried, on all your food. Use them in your cooking. Steep them in some boiling water for a delicious and nutritious herbal tea. Eat them fresh out of the garden. Bask in their fragrance, their texture, their flavour, their *energy*!

The purpose of this nutrition chapter is to help you rediscover what food is all about. It is a glorious thing and food can heal us, if we allow ourselves to be guided by our instincts.

INTUITION AND A HAPPY BODY

This is a little reminder to you that exercise and body movement is also vital to maintaining good health and happiness. You may be surprised to learn that the amount of exercise each body needs varies greatly. The same principles I discussed for food, also apply for exercise. Use your intuition, be gentle on yourself and enjoy it! If you aren't enjoying the activity, drop it, because it isn't doing you any favours.

Some people prefer to go for a leisurely stroll every day, and that is enough for their body. Others do two hours at the gym, lifting weights and pushing their bodies to the limit. It doesn't matter what the exercise or activity is, as long as you are enjoying it.

Our muscles need to be worked, so they can maintain proper function. And physical exercise has the added benefit of releasing all those lovely feel-good chemicals in our body like endorphins. Without overwhelming yourself with too many changes too soon, slowly and enjoyably welcome some changes to your daily and weekly physical activity until you find a balance that makes you happy.

Do you know, I have been so vigilant with my spiritual and mental health these past couple of years, but not so on point with my physical health. And I can feel it. My spiritual and mental states are the best they have ever been – ever! But my physical body is struggling, and I know it's because it is hardly doing any movement. I know that my one hour per week of social badminton, which is super fun and a good workout, isn't quite enough movement for my body, right now. My body needs more. And my intuition led me to yoga.

I have had an ongoing spine issue for years, and I was advised by a medical professional that yoga would only hurt my back even more and cause me more pain. As the words came out of his mouth, I heard my own soul whisper softly but firmly: *no, it won't*.

For almost twelve months I felt terribly unfit. I knew that yoga would be exactly what I needed, but I was too afraid I would be wrong and my doctor would be right.

My doctor is someone I trust. He has been the only person able to help me manage my back pain to the point where it is pretty much non-existent – every other professional and doctor I had seen prior to meeting him, told me I had to learn to live with the pain. He proved them all wrong. But would *he* be the one who was wrong, this time?

Finally, I took a deep breath and decided to give yoga a go. I could almost hear my favourite doctor tut-tutting and shaking his head at me. This was a big deal!

To begin, I committed to practicing yoga three times a week and for the first week, I blitzed it. But then I didn't go for three weeks, not because my back was hurting, but because I just couldn't find the time or the inclination. It's all about balance, you see.

When I released all expectations of myself around exercise and physical fitness and decided I would be happy with going whenever I could manage it, my motivation increased. Sometimes I'll now go to two or three classes in one week and sometimes there will be weeks in between visits. I'm now totally okay with that.

The breathlessness I had been struggling with for months is not as noticeable. My lethargy is decreasing. My back pain has decreased even more. I am much more flexible, even only after a few short weeks.

But the biggest unexpected bonus of attending yoga for me? I can now look at myself in the mirrors of the yoga room, with very little clothing on and sweat pouring off me, my beetroot-red face gazing back at me, without cringing. Through exercise and meditation (yoga being a form of meditation) I am learning to love myself more.

Through this exercise, I can *feel* the energy buzzing through my whole body, as my heart pumps a little faster and the blood starts rushing through my veins and oh my goodness, it feels incredible!

Exercise is the missing piece of my current happiness puzzle. I just had to find the right type of exercise that was not only physically beneficial, but super enjoyable as well.

The next thing on my exercise wish-list? My intuition is steering me towards kick-boxing and dancing. What is on your exercise wish-list? Be bold and brave, and give it a go.

A gentle reminder for you: whatever piece of your puzzle you are currently working on, whether it be physical, mental, emotional or spiritual health, please go gently. Don't try and create a massive overhaul of all aspects of your life, all at once. You will become quickly overwhelmed by all the changes and will possibly find that none of them can be maintained long term.

If it takes a year or two to work out what it is you love to do for physical activity, and how often you love to do it, then take those couple of years in your stride and enjoy every minute! Then, when you are feeling like that part of your life is working well for you, pick another area to work on. Gently does it.

What physical activity is your intuition steering you towards, right now? Do you feel like your body needs some vigorous movement, or some gentle stretching? Do you feel like your body needs to be moving around in the great outdoors? Or does your body need to be quietly resting? Do you feel like you need to go it alone? Or do you need to recruit some help for motivation and guidance?

Let your body and your intuition guide you, and exercise will no longer be a chore. When you trust and act on your intuition, that inner knowing, all guilt is set free. No longer will you feel guilty for resting when you need to, or for saying no to an invitation so you can go for a run. Intuition and a happy, healthy body go hand in hand.

THE GREAT AND POWERFUL MIND

Your mind is a very powerful part of your body and it also needs love and care. Exercising your mind and developing your intellect are important for your overall good health and happiness. Your mind needs to be worked, so it too can function well.

How do you work your mind? Play board games, do crosswords, have a deep and meaningful conversation with someone, write in a journal or diary, study, take up a new hobby or interest, do a puzzle.

Now don't get me wrong – the mind needs exercise, but the mind doesn't control your body. Many people think that having a sharp and clever mind is the ultimate goal for happiness and success. To me, this is a misconception. Yes, a sharp and clever mind is certainly a bonus and our mind needs attention, just like every other part of our body, but it is not the engine that drives us.

The mind is an extremely powerful thing and if you let it, can take charge of your body and this is often when you lose touch with your soul-self. I have lost count of the number of times a person has come to me for help because their mind is running on overdrive, to the point where it is seriously affecting their health and happiness. Some gentle energy healing, combined with some simple techniques to quieten the mind, has seen some powerful and often immediate results.

A mind that is working all day and all night is not a happy, healthy mind. A mind that knows its place and works when you need it and quietens itself when you don't, is a happy and healthy mind which can, in turn, bring immeasurable overall happiness.

Imagine your muscles being worked all day and night, for days and weeks and months at a time. Those muscles would be worn out and unhappy. We generally have a great balance when it comes to exercise and relaxation but when it comes to our minds, we are always working them round the clock.

In my experience, an overworked mind can cause sleeplessness, stress, depression, anxiety, anger and frustration, confusion and brain fog, among many other things. A sluggish and bored mind can also have a detrimental effect, but this is a rarity now that we all have such busy lifestyles. Your mind needs variety, which is why the activities above will come in handy because they exercise different parts of your brain.

MINDFULNESS ACTIVITIES

So how do you quieten your mind? Meditation! I can't stress enough, *meditate meditate meditate!*

It will help restore the balance between mind, body and soul. Another great way I like to quieten my mind is to escape the everyday and spend some time in nature. And if you need a quick fix or don't have time to get out of town, pop on your headphones so you can listen to some soothing sounds of nature on your music app, then get outside, get your bare feet in the grass or dirt, then close your eyes. Your soul will be taken on a ride through nature, as the music in your ears and the feel of the Earth beneath your feet quietens your mind and transports you away from reality for a little while. Even something as simple as going for a walk around your neighbourhood can quieten your mind, if you are doing it mindfully and really soaking up your surroundings through all of your senses.

Another little tip that may help keep your mind in check: whenever you are doing mundane, everyday chores, practise focusing on the chore for as long as you can, rather than allowing yourself to daydream or to run those pesky to do lists through your head. If your thoughts stray, gently guide them back to the task at hand.

Let's say you're washing dishes – listen to the water as it sloshes around in the sink, feel the warmth of the water on your hands, watch the sudsy bubbles popping and moving and glistening in the light. This is what is commonly known as mindfulness; the act of deliberately paying attention to the present moment.

Don't just focus your attention on the task you are doing; focus as many of your senses as possible on the task. This will help you to keep your mind still. Practice makes permanent! The more you do this, the easier it becomes.

As I have previously mentioned, your body is your temple. This statement is used a lot, but I don't think many people stop and think about what it means. You only have one body in this lifetime, and this temple of yours deserves to be respected and loved. If you feel like it is failing you for any reason; illness, injury, or it just doesn't look 'good' to you, all the more reason to nurture it. Love it, provide it with fuel, keep it active, stay positive, and your body will respond with joy!

19

OTHER PRACTICAL TIPS AND TRICKS

'Integrate some self-care routines into your everyday life, and your life will transform.'

Do you need a few other self-care suggestions? This chapter will walk you through some other therapies and everyday practices that can help you.

MASSAGE

Who doesn't love a good massage? Many people crave physical touch. Whether you are in a relationship or you are single, the need for your body to be touched can be overwhelmingly strong. And I'm not talking about sexual touch here, although this type of touch and intimacy is also vital for our overall wellbeing and happiness.

Over the years, I have had many massages and have always enjoyed them, but since discovering energy and spirituality I am now able to appreciate the full effect of a good massage. Combine the skilled touch of a massage therapist with the energetic exchange taking place, and you have yourself one extremely potent experience.

There are many different styles of massage, so if you are looking for something a little bit different to your usual remedial massage therapy, perhaps consider trying one of the following styles. These are some of my favourite massage therapies, but there are many others. Do some research to learn of different massage therapists in your local area and what they have to offer.

KAHUNA MASSAGE

Kahuna massage originates from Hawaii. During a Kahuna massage, the practitioner will use their hands, elbows, fingers and forearms to rhythmically and intentionally massage your full body. Your Kahuna therapist works intuitively and lovingly. Your Kahuna therapist will lose all sense of reality, as he or she connects with your energy and your emotions to give you what you need at that moment in time.

Your therapist is trained to harness the essence of the aloha spirit of Hawaiian culture; she will focus solely on you and your entire being with nothing but love and compassion in her heart. The rhythmic, hula-like movements of your therapist, as she glides around the table, are believed to create harmony between you and your therapist.

I have been very lucky to experience what a Kahuna massage has to offer and this experience was like nothing I have ever experienced before. It wasn't until after the massage had finished, that I realised just how much my body, mind and soul had been craving this experience.

It was a healing experience through loving touch, muscle relaxation and bucket-loads of channelled love and acceptance. A Kahuna massage is an empowering and sensual experience. It is the ultimate treat for your body and your soul.

ABHYANGA

Abhyanga is a traditional Ayurvedic warm oil massage. Ayurvedic medicine, also known as Ayurveda, is one of the oldest holistic healing systems, originating in India. Ayurveda is one of the most fascinating and resonating healing systems I have ever encountered; so much so, I seriously considered studying to become a qualified Ayurvedic Practitioner a few years ago.

If you are interested in learning more about Ayurveda, I have included an Ayurvedic reference in the back of this book for you to begin exploring this wondrous system because I believe it can help everyone achieve better health and happiness. I have integrated elements of Ayurveda into my everyday life on and off over the past few years, with great success.

One of my favourites is Abhyanga. You might like to visit your nearest Ayurvedic Practitioner to experience this incredible massage style, or you can get some oil and do it yourself; there are significant benefits from both options.

The warm oil used during Abhyanga is medicated with herbs. Different oil blends are used for different people, depending on the individual's constitution or body type according to Ayurvedic Medicine. Your therapist, who is not only a skilled massage therapist but also a qualified Ayurvedic Practitioner, will assess you prior to your massage so they can be sure to use the right oil blend and the right techniques for you. Abhyanga is safe for everyone including children, pregnant women and the elderly. It promotes overall wellness and nourishment for your entire being.

If you would prefer to do it yourself, here is a basic introduction from a good friend of mine who practices Abhyanga as part of her daily morning ritual, and who is well-versed in Ayurveda. This has been an integral part of her self-care routine for a long time and she swears by it!

She recently guided me through performing my own Abhyanga

and, much like the Kahuna massage, it was life-changing. It was an empowering and nurturing experience, and it was all the more special because I wasn't relying on anyone else to make me feel nurtured and loved. I was doing it all myself!

You need to allow yourself time to work through this ritualistic practice of self-massage; don't rush it. You must prioritise your own happiness and wellbeing.

I was gifted an oil blend to sample, but if you don't know where to start with this, you can either just use your favourite base massage oil (olive oil, sesame oil, etc), or you can infuse this base oil with some of your favourite herbs, or you can purchase a ready-made Ayurvedic oil blend. An important note: if you are pregnant or if you have any pre-existing health issues, please consult your health care practitioner before using any herbal oil blends.

ABHYANGA SELF-MASSAGE

Your Abhyanga can be performed while sitting or standing, naked or partly clothed, and with or without relaxing music playing in the background. You will be working your way from your head, down to your feet and you can use as little or as much oil as you like.

As you work your way through the following steps, it is important that you use the power of your thoughts to enhance this act of self-care. Set an intention before you start, that *you are dedicating this time to loving and nurturing yourself*. And throughout the massage, hold on to thoughts of self-love and self-compassion.

Gently heat your oil until it is at a warm temperature that won't burn you or cause any discomfort. To begin, dip your fingertips into your oil and repeat this as often as you need, throughout the massage.

Slowly and gently circle your fingertips on the crown of your head, working out from there in circular strokes until you are circling and massaging your entire scalp. Take your time.

Using your fingertips, massage in small circular motions on your face; focussing on forehead, temples, cheeks (especially just under your eye sockets) and jaw. Don't press too hard. Be gentle and loving.

Massage your ears. Include the entire surface area of both ears, including the ear lobes.

Working your way down your body, gently massage your arms with long, gentle strokes of your hands. Massage your shoulders and elbows in circular motions.

Massage your hands, paying attention to the full length of your fingers and in between your fingers.

Massage your chest and breasts, gently and intuitively.

Massage your abdomen in long circular movements, moving up on the right side, then across and down the left side.

Keep working down your body, massaging your legs in long, gentle strokes and your knees in a circular motion.

Finally, massage your feet; top and bottom and all toes.

You should not feel like you have exerted yourself, you should feel beautifully relaxed and peaceful. If you do feel like this was a big effort for you, you have applied too much pressure or moved too quickly.

When you have finished, leave the oil on your skin for anywhere between five to twenty minutes. This is especially important if you are using herbal-infused oil, as this gives the potency of the herbs a chance to penetrate your skin and work their magic.

Wipe off excess oil and then enjoy a warm bath or shower to remove the remaining oil from your skin. It was explained to me the reason for this being, the oil draws out the toxins in your body. Therefore if the oil remains on your skin, so do the toxins. Wash the oil and the toxins away, gently pat yourself dry with a clean towel, then go and enjoy your day!

I was advised it is best to perform Abhyanga first thing in the morning, however you will still greatly benefit from doing it any time of the day or night. If you can do this for yourself at least twice weekly, you will achieve the best outcome.

It doesn't need to be a full body Ayurvedic massage that you give yourself. Any form of self-massage is beneficial! When I give myself a massage, I find that just by focusing on one of the following areas is enough to help ease so many things like anxiety, stress, headaches, stomach upsets, insomnia, low moods, and other general aches and pains.

FOOT MASSAGE

Give your ankles, your feet and your toes a really good massage with your favourite lotion or oil. If you have someone handy who can do this for you, enlist their help! A ten-minute foot massage can turn your mood from tired and grumpy to calm and content.

ABDOMINAL MASSAGE

Gently or firmly massage your abdomen in smooth, circular strokes, moving up your right side, then across and down the left side. This movement follows the path of the large intestine or the colon, and stimulates digestion and healthy bowel movements. A healthy digestive system can have a massive impact on your overall health.

EAR MASSAGE

Don't discount the value of a good ear massage! There are acupressure points in your ears that, just like the points in your feet, cover almost your entire physical and energetic body and all organs.

When you are massaging your ears, it is like massaging your whole being.

There are also many nerve endings in your ear lobes, so the skin on this part of your body is particularly sensitive and responsive. Treat yourself to a short or a long ear massage and you will be recharging your entire body.

Any type of massage works towards relieving pain and tension, increasing circulation and achieving deep relaxation. Massage can help you heal physically and emotionally.

Energetically speaking, a massage also has the potential to stimulate your soul energy and reconnect you with your inner-self. Through massage, your chakras can be cleansed and balanced and you can release not only emotional tension, but energetic congestion as well.

Massage also stimulates the meridians within your body, as it works on the meridian endpoints through acupressure. The next time you experience a massage, whether it be from a professional or yourself, set some intentions beforehand for what you would like to receive or achieve from the massage. Then relax and surrender to the experience. Think of it from an energetic or spiritual point of view, and notice how much more powerful the massage becomes.

As you can see, there is a wide array of massage choices waiting for you to explore! I would like to finish up this discussion on massage with sharing a little insider's tip: many massage therapists are also trained energy healers who often don't promote their healing services. So don't be afraid to ask around! You could make your massage therapist's day, because many are not yet feeling brave enough to put themselves out there as a healer.

The more people in the community openly seeking a therapist who offers massage *and* energy healing services, the sooner these skilful and soulful therapists can feel confident to step into their own true self. Our world needs this so much!

CLINICAL HYPNOTHERAPY

Many people associate hypnosis with a performer on stage, making the audience do amusing and sometimes zany things. Hypnosis is not just something to entertain us. It is a real therapy, conducted by qualified practitioners helping people with a wide range of issues of the mind.

An eighteenth-century German physician and healer by the name of Franz Anton Mesmer developed a technique to *mesmerise* his patients to help them heal. This technique was later adapted by James Braid, a surgeon from Manchester and it is believed that Dr Braid coined the term hypnosis, after the Greek god of sleep, *Hypnos*. Hypnosis, for a very long time, was considered a tool for spiritual fulfilment so it didn't gain much support or respect from the medical community. It wasn't until the mid-1900s that hypnosis was scientifically studied using modern-day medicine and science and from then, slowly began to earn the respect it deserves.

So what is hypnotherapy and how does it relate to energy healing? I had a chat with Dr Nicholas Chantler AM, a qualified clinical hypnotherapist, so I could learn more about this intriguing therapy.

Hypnotherapy is the process of using hypnosis to help resolve problems of a mental or psychological nature. What is hypnosis? Dr Chantler explains that hypnosis taps into the subconscious mind, where every single experience you have ever been part of is stored.

Let's briefly discuss the three different layers or levels of the mind, from a neuroscience perspective, being the scientific study of the nervous system and its functions. The surface or top layer of your mind is your conscious, and this is the layer accessed when you are in an awake and lucid state. All memories you can recall while in an awake state are stored here.

Your subconscious is the next layer of the mind – the layer accessed during hypnosis – and everything you have ever experienced in your life is stored here. This is your memory bank in its entirety.

The unconscious is the final layer of the mind, and this controls the part of the nervous system responsible for involuntary bodily functions, such as breathing and the heartbeat. If a person is knocked unconscious, they still breathe – they are still alive – and this is thanks to the unconscious.

So all those memories you have that play through your mind from time to time, of past experiences and relationships – they are all stored in your conscious and are always accessible. But what about those memories you can't recall? Those things you have experienced or learned, but have forgotten?

Those memories you have tucked away, usually as a means of self-protection or self-preservation, are still there in your mind. They haven't magically disappeared. These memories are all stored in your subconscious.

A clinical hypnotherapist helps you access your subconscious so you can heal from a range of issues including depression, anxiety, phobias and fears, addictions and any other mental, emotional or psychological issues. They do this with a range of tools and techniques to put the conscious mind in a state of complete rest.

When this top layer of the mind is still, the subconscious mind can be accessed; this is what defines hypnosis – the act of accessing the subconscious. The therapist then supports you as you access memories appropriate to the root cause of the issue you are dealing with.

Because of the nature of this experience, it is crucial for you to trust your therapist to achieve the best results. The more you trust your therapist, the more you will let your guard down and relax.

Hypnotherapy is now widely recognised throughout the world as an effective therapy for healing the mind. From Dr Chantler's experience, not only is he as a practitioner tapping into the mind of the person, he believes he is also tapping into their soul-self.

I tend to think these deeper layers of the mind are more than just what neuroscience says they are. From an energetic perspective, the mind – through its varying levels of consciousness – is connecting and communicating with other energies around us.

There are, of course, many clinical hypnotherapists who would dismiss this suggestion, however Dr Chantler firmly believes the act of hypnosis is so much more than unlocking the mind. He suggests the mind is not something that resides only in your head. He suggests the mind exists in your head, around your head, and beyond. He believes, through witnessing hundreds of client sessions over twenty years of practice, that hypnosis heals the mind and the soul.

AUTOSUGGESTION

An alternative to hypnotherapy, and something you can do for yourself, is a technique known as *autosuggestion*. The practice of autosuggestion is based on similar principles to hypnotherapy – accessing the subconscious mind to generate new, healthier thought patterns and releasing old, unhealthy thought patterns or habits.

That's the simplified definition. Or, an even simpler definition: you will rewire your brain.

Intrigued? Me too!

Autosuggestion will only work if you are in a deep state of relaxation. Ideally, your brain needs to be in that lovely theta state

– the point where you are very nearly, but not quite asleep. You quieten your conscious mind, so your subconscious can shine through.

Here are some suggestions for the best time to practice autosuggestion to ensure you are deeply relaxed:

- When you are laying in bed, just before sleep.

- When you are laying in bed, first thing in the morning when you wake.

- After you have taken a nice warm shower.

- After you have enjoyed a cup of tea or another comforting drink of choice.

- While resting and listening to some soothing music.

- After working through the breathing meditation from the meditation chapter of this book.

- When you are immersed in nature, with nothing but the sounds of nature all around you.

- Any other time of the day, or other activity that you love to do, to achieve considerable relaxation.

It doesn't matter what you do, as long as your method is consistent and you feel deeply relaxed afterwards. This is your personal ritual, and this is step one of your autosuggestion practice.

If you use the same relaxation technique each time it creates a habit, reinforcing the whole concept behind autosuggestion – reprogram the mind through repetitive behaviour.

Once you have established step one of your autosuggestion practice and you are feeling super relaxed and calm, you are now ready for step two. It is now time to chant your way through a positive affirmation specific to the issue you are working on. Here are some useful suggestions for positive affirmations:

- *'Yes I can,'* (helpful for confidence)

- *'I am comfortable with heights,'* (helpful for various fears or phobias)

- *'I am peaceful,'* (helpful for anxiety)

- *'My self-control is perfect,'* (helpful for addictions)

Or, create your own positive affirmations tailored to your personal needs. Be specific, be concise. Your positive affirmation must be in first person and in present tense. Example: *I am*, or *I can*, or *I do*.

Repeat your positive affirmation either in your mind or aloud *at least three times, preferably more*. Repetition is important – repeat repeat repeat!

Having the affirmation written down, so you can read it from the page, can be helpful. Or an alternative is to have images in front of you – images which reinforce your affirmation – for you to look at during your autosuggestion practice.

As you are working through step two of your autosuggestion practice, put as much emotion and love as you can behind the positive affirmation – this will help immensely. The more you can *feel* your affirmation, the faster it will be ingrained in your subconscious.

Do these two steps every single day for at least a few weeks, perhaps even months, and you will retrain or reprogram your subconscious to think and respond in healthier, more productive ways. Once you are happy you have achieved your desired outcome, you can start the whole process again with a new positive affirmation as your main focus (while being consistent with step one – maintain the same ritual, always). It is best to only work on one positive affirmation at a time.

Autosuggestion – much like hypnotherapy – is great for combatting addictions and other bad habits, phobias and fears, negative self-talk, anxiety, and other issues of the mind, but you need to be persistent, consistent and habitual with this practice.

You know by now the power of your thoughts, the power of emotion and the power of love from a spiritual or energetic perspective. So not only are you rewiring your brain to behave in healthier ways through autosuggestion, you are reprogramming your soul energy too. You are energetically releasing the bad stuff and replacing it with good stuff. Autosuggestion (and perhaps even hypnotherapy) could therefore be considered another form of energy medicine.

Your mind can heal, just like every other part of your being. Healthy mind, healthy body, healthy soul. It's all connected; through healing one aspect of yourself, you heal them all. It is worth the effort, because you are working towards a healthier and *happier* you.

BATH TIME

One of the easiest and most accessible ways to practice self-care is to have a bath! Throw in some Epsom salts to enhance your bathing experience. Epsom salts are magnesium bath salts or flakes that can be purchased from any good health shop or from your local supermarket. Add your favourite essential oils, or just toss in something from your pantry like Himalayan pink salt or apple cider vinegar. Pop on some soothing music or grab your favourite book, hop in the tub and allow your body to soak in the warm water.

A bath is very therapeutic because it allows you to take yourself away from the everyday and unwind. Water has very healing properties because it is Earth energy. Combined with the other additions mentioned above, it can be a detoxifying experience for your body and a spiritually cleansing experience for your soul.

If you want to dramatically ramp up the healing properties of a bath, do some visualisation: imagine, as the bath water is drained away afterwards, it takes with it all your old, negative, used energy. It is sending it back to the Earth, where it will be recycled and renewed.

You will get out of that bath feeling like a million dollars! Or you will feel like you have just run a marathon and need to go to bed immediately. Either result will mean the bath has served you well. Keep well-hydrated after a detoxifying bath by drinking lots of water. You are supporting and nourishing your body – hooray for you!

Do you want to go next-level with your bath? Try float therapy on for size. Picture this: you are in a sound-proof, dark, cosy and warm space and you are floating weightlessly in a giant tub of warm, salty water.

The water solution is denser than normal water, thanks to the addition of several hundred kilograms of Epsom salt (magnesium sulphate). This salty water solution will keep you buoyant on top of the water and even if you fall asleep, you will still float.

The water around you and the air above you is body-temperature, leaving you feeling like you are suspended in space. There is no stimulation of any of the senses; you experience total sensory deprivation. You will escape the outside world, and perhaps even your body, for an hour or two.

If you are claustrophobic like me, don't let this deter you! There are float tanks and float rooms available, so if you don't like the idea of being closed in a tank that isn't much bigger than your own body, find yourself a float room. If I had to choose one word to describe a float, I would choose: *heaven*!

SPACE CLEARING

If you are focusing solely on the self-care of your own body, mind and soul and still don't feel great, this usually means *the space around you* needs some tender love and care. Your home, your workplace, anywhere you spend a lot of time each day, also needs to be maintained energetically.

Sometimes negative emotions and other low energy can congest the space around you, rather than inside you. This might result in the energy of a bedroom (or any room), an entire home, school or workplace feeling heavy, suffocating, and even sometimes a little eerie if it's been there building up for long enough. Sometimes it might only be noticeable in one room, or you'll feel it through the whole building.

Here are some tips on cleansing the energy around you, which is just as important as keeping your own soul energy clear.

De-clutter your life! Here are some suggestions:

- *Digital media.* Unfollow or unlike those social media pages or, dare I say it, friends who no longer bring you joy. Instead of scrolling past or deleting all those subscription emails clogging up your inbox, click on the appropriate link and unsubscribe. Delete any contacts, messages and photos from your mobile phone that are now obsolete.

- *Around the home.* Clean out your pantry and your wardrobe. I know, it's a huge job! But trust me, it is so worth it. Go through your house and pile up all your unwanted possessions and either have a garage sale, stick them on an online marketplace or go to a local car boot sale and sell them. Or donate to a local charity. Or re-gift to family and friends. In the garden, pick a little spot that is easy to work with and make it something special. Clear the overgrowth, prune the plants, get creative and give it some love.

- *Your work space.* Tidy your desk and draws, then add something special to brighten the space. Maybe flowers in a vase, a special crystal or gemstone, photos of loved ones or artwork on the wall. Put your special stamp on the space; make it yours.

- *Friendships and Relationships.* It is okay to let go of relationships no longer serving you. People come and go from our lives, and this happens for many reasons. I believe that relationships serve a purpose; they are part of your soul journey. Some relationships are meant to be life-long and others are destined to be short and sweet. Relationships teach you lessons, and they heal you and enrich your life. When you move on from relationships that no longer feel right, you are clearing a space for new, fresh relationships to enter your life and these new souls will help you continue to grow and flourish.

As you de-clutter your life, send out a little, *'Thank you and goodbye'* to whatever it is you are removing from your life, because at some stage, it did serve a purpose. De-cluttering is very liberating!

The act of de-cluttering is the act of releasing all the old, stagnant energy from your life. If it has been a long time since you had a good clean out in any or all the above areas of your life, I highly recommend making this a priority. You'll feel better afterwards, I promise.

In the words of a famous animated movie: *let it go!*

Enlist the help of some simple space-cleansing tools!

Just as you would cleanse and strengthen your own soul energy, you can do much the same for the energy around you using a range of simple tools. I use all of these space-clearing tools regularly with great success. Pick one (or several) and give it a try!

- *Sound vibrations* such as wind chimes or your favourite music.

- *Indoor plants* not only improve the air quality of your indoor space, they also energetically cleanse and strengthen the space, too.

- *Furniture made from natural products* such as wood or stone bring the Earth's energy into your space.

- *Natural scents* such as aromatic essential oils or flowers from the garden.

- *Décor made from natural products* such as crystals and gemstones, also bring the Earth's energy into your space.

- *Natural light* from the sun.

- *Smoke* from a candle, incense or smudging herbs.

- *Fresh air!* Open the windows and doors frequently.

- *Redecorate!* You'll be surprised how effective shifting some furniture around can be. The placement of furniture can greatly affect the feel or energy in a space.

- *Colours* are an important energetic element in any room or building. Add a splash of new colour, whether it be a vibrant and bold colour or an earthy hue, any colour additions to your space will help shift the energy.

As with all energy work, intention is everything here. So if you are doing something to cleanse or strengthen the energy in the space around you, be sure to hold that exact intention in your mind as you do it. The energy of your thoughts will add to the energy of, say, the music, and the benefits will be much more noticeable.

If you are using crystals, plants, wood, or any other natural element to clear your space, make sure to cleanse their energy every now and then as well. As these Earth products absorb the negative energy, they will need to release it at some stage. So pop them outside on the grass so they can cleanse and recharge. Or you can use the other cleansing options discussed in the *Crystal Healing* section of this book, if you prefer.

While we are on the subject of space clearing, let's have a discussion on the importance of cleansing the energy in your children's bedrooms. Is your child afraid of her bedroom at night? Has she ever told you there is something in her room? Does she seem quite unsettled when she's in her bed or in her bedroom? If this is the case, the energy in your child's room is too dense and needs some clearing. You can use any or all of the previous suggestions to clear the energy in your child's bedroom.

Another wonderful tip specific to children, is to introduce them to dream catchers. Both my children have dream catchers in their bedrooms. If a parent ever approaches me asking for advice on their child not being comfortable in their bedroom – including issues like sleeplessness, night terrors and fear – the first thing I suggest is a dream catcher for their bedroom and every single time it works a treat.

Let your child choose where she would like the dream catcher to hang in her bedroom, because children are very intuitive. Then teach her how it works: All bad dreams, sad feelings, or strange energies will be caught by her dream catcher. Her dream catcher will protect her and her bedroom. To empty her dream catcher, she must take it outside whenever she needs and hold it out at arm's length, to let the wind and the sun take away all the bad stuff. It will then be ready to hang back in her bedroom, so it can continue to take extra special care of her.

Space clearing is something that needs to be done on a regular basis. If you are vigilant with your space clearing, you will have a happier and healthier environment around you and your loved ones. And you don't need to go to extremes! By introducing even just one of the techniques above, you will be making a difference.

THE FIVE SENSES

If you are lucky enough to be blessed with all five of your senses, I encourage you to indulge all of them regularly. This simple act of self-care is something you can do anytime, anywhere.

Sight, sound, smell, touch, taste. Your five senses stimulate and teach your body. They are constantly feeding signals to your body, then being metabolized by you. To truly nurture your body, consider indulging all your senses.

- *Sight – Visual stimulation.* If you see something that catches your attention as you go about your day, stop for a minute and see it. Pay close attention. Appreciate its beauty.

- *Sound – Aural stimulation.* Listen to music that makes your heart sing. Listen to the sounds of nature. Listen to silence.

- *Smell – Scent stimulation.* Flowers, essential oils, food. Inhale slowly, and feel the scent radiating through your body. Burn some good quality incense or dried herbs, not only does it smell incredible, the smoke will also energetically cleanse the room.

- *Touch – Physical stimulation.* Bare skin against another pure energy source such as a loved one, a pet, the Earth. Snuggle with a favourite blanket. Treat yourself to a massage.

- *Taste – Flavour stimulation.* Sweet, sour, salty, astringent, bitter, pungent. Eat a variety of foods to make your taste buds explode with excitement.

If we dull one sense, it heightens the others. Try closing your eyes when listening to your favourite cd, or when you are hugging a loved one.

Seek out things that stimulate all five senses, and your body will respond with joy.

≺≺≺ ≻≻≻

Self-care in all forms – energy, spiritual, emotional, physical and mental – is crucial to a happy and fulfilled life. The more you can mix it up, the more you will benefit. Being able to switch off and completely surrender while a skilled therapist works their magic on you, is a treat everyone should have the pleasure of experiencing.

Sometimes you will need to enlist the help of someone else to support, love and nourish you and other times it is necessary to take your self-care into your own hands. Sometimes, we need to let go and let someone else carry us for a little while, and other times we step up and do it alone. Finding that balance between reaching out and retreating is so important, so let your instincts guide you.

Now you have no excuses. Make a few changes here and there! Try on a few of my suggestions for size.

Find what works for you. Integrate some self-care routines into your everyday life, and your life will transform. You will find inner peace, you will learn to love yourself and this, in turn, will raise your spiritual awareness. You will feel more connected to yourself and to others. And you may just find that your connectedness to your soul energy is enhanced and you will clearly hear all the whisperings of guidance and support it is constantly sending you.

You will be fierce. And you will be happy. That sounds like a pretty awesome way to live life!

20

MANIFESTATION OF YOUR DREAMS

'Reassess. Recalibrate. Make a change.
Visualise. Keep working hard.'

You have the power to make stuff happen. Whatever it is you desire, you can make it a reality. This is what we call manifestation, by turning the abstract into the actual.

Many techniques already mentioned in this book are used for manifestation of dreams and goals. Vision boards, positive affirmations, meditations, healings, pretty much any spiritual practice can result in the manifestation of your deepest desires. Please don't just take my word for it, try it out for yourself!

You are in total control of your life and your path, don't ever be afraid to make stuff happen. There is just one condition: please always ask that the manifestation is for your highest good and greatest joy. By including this simple and succinct statement in your manifestation practices, you are ensuring that whatever happens, happens with your absolute best interests as priority. Therefore if what you are working towards doesn't eventuate, or it seems to take forever to achieve, know there is either something better on the horizon waiting for you, or there are more lessons yet to be learned.

When you are manifesting something good in your life, you need to remember a few key points:

- Refer to it in the present tense: *it is*, rather than *it will*.

- *Imagine how you will feel* when your desire is a reality – then really *connect* with this feeling in the present moment.

- *Focus on creating the positive*, rather than eliminating the negative: *my body is healthy* (the focus here is 'healthy'), rather than *I am not sick* (the focus here is 'sick').

- *Be consistent and persistent*: every day, give your manifestation your attention – even a few seconds is better than nothing, for example glancing at your vision board as you walk past.

- *If you meditate regularly, add a simple mantra* of your manifestation to your meditation practice.

- *Be open to receiving a whole lot of lessons* along the way to achieving your manifestation: these lessons are often why some manifestations take time to achieve. Notice the lessons! This will keep things moving forward for you.

- *Keep trusting in yourself* and in the Universe: if you *believe* it will happen with every ounce of your being, you will experience amazing things.

I would like to share with you a couple of my own personal stories involving manifestation, in the hopes that something, somewhere in these shared stories will resonate with you and inspire you to give manifesting a go, with your eyes wide open.

I have for years now, struggled with the feeling that I'm not financially secure. I used to constantly worry about money. And there have been times over the years, where cash flow has been so tight for my family, it has caused me great stress. I have now turned my financial situation around. I am achieving prosperity, to ease the financial pressures my family and I constantly face.

I decided I was going to use manifestation techniques to achieve this goal of mine a couple of years ago. I collected statements of all my financial debt. I wrote on all of them in big red ink, *paid in full*. Then I filed them all in a folder, also labelled *paid in full*.

I crossed out the bank balance of my current everyday savings account statement and wrote *one hundred thousand dollars* as the balance and sat this on my desk, so I could see it every day and send positive energy to my goal.

I have read books on finance and budgeting. I have expressed gratitude a million times over, for what I have already been provided with financially. I have done meditations for abundance and prosperity. I have used daily positive affirmations for financial abundance. I have asked for spiritual guidance on what else I need to do to achieve prosperity.

I have worked for years now on this manifestation of my goal and, right now, I am in much less debt than I was this time last year. This achievement alone is huge for me and I now consider myself as being in a prosperous environment. It is very encouraging and I am extremely grateful.

This manifestation of mine is slow going, but I can see how far I've come and I can see my goal right there in front of me.

Sometimes my family and I struggle financially and life does get tough. But the hard times are now shorter-lived and after these hard times, I can always see *why* we were dealt that particular hand.

Now, let's keep it real, even though I can see the *why*, I don't always agree with it or like it. Sometimes the *why* makes me mad. But my eyes are open. I'm under no false impressions and my blinkers are off.

I once attended a gathering where ritual and meditation were used, with the intention of releasing energetic blocks and healing. We were asked to focus on something in our life we are currently working on, struggling with, ready to let go of, and so on. My attention was instinctively drawn to money. I had a little chuckle to myself – we meet again, old friend!

We were then led through a guided meditation and I had a profound moment of clarity: why do I feel guilty for wanting lots of money? I am comfortable asking for an abundance of love in my life. I am comfortable asking for an abundance of good health in my life. These wants are reasonable and aren't from a place of greed. So why did I feel so guilty when wishing for an abundance of money? Love is energy. Happiness is energy. And in that moment, it dawned on me: *money is also energy*.

Money is not something to be ashamed of. Money is not something to feel burdened or controlled by. Money, as with everything, is energy and the second I made that (in hindsight, *blindingly* obvious) connection, I felt a shift. I felt my relationship to money instantly change like it has never done before.

I *am* worthy of financial abundance. Finally I can say this without feeling ashamed. I want lots of money, and that's not a bad thing. It's a very good thing! Oh, the things I will do when I have financial abundance! Help my family, help my children, help my community, and help myself. No greed here, just love.

The lessons I have learned throughout this manifestation of financial abundance are priceless. I have learned so much about trust and about priorities. My family is now closer, because of these experiences we have had involving money. We have surfaced from the other side, when times have been extremely tough, stronger and united.

I now have a healthier appreciation of money. It no longer controls me or hogs the limelight as much as it used to. I acknowledge that I still have work to do.

There are still some pesky, old, self-sabotaging habits currently being dealt with, but the important thing is that I have acknowledged them and I'm putting in the work needed to release them. Sometimes, that can be the hardest part of the healing journey – recognition of the lesson. Once recognised, it can be dealt with.

I do want to be prosperous. But I also want the lessons and the healings I am receiving along the way. I am so thankful for everything I already have, and I am working hard to earn more money. With love in my heart, I am open to receiving money by any and all means, and I am appreciating my own worth by spending money on just me, from time to time. I can see the shift happening. My efforts are paying off and I'm making sure I celebrate the small, yet very significant wins as much as I celebrate the big wins.

I say again, no greed here; just a heart and soul full of love, thankful for everything that comes my way. I trust that everything happens for a reason and that I am well on my way to achieving my goal of prosperity.

If these words on money are striking a chord with you, please know that you, too, can achieve abundance in all areas of your life through manifestation. Say it with me:

I am open to receiving abundance in all areas of my life, for my highest good.

I believe manifestations are real. Some people may say it is sheer luck. Others may say it is simply a result of hard work. Perhaps it's a combination of all the above? Does it matter? What matters, is that you believe. You believe in yourself and in your ability to make things happen. This will give you strength and courage.

I believed I would beat my illness, and I did. I believed I would turn my humble little bookkeeping business into a thriving entity, and I did. I believe. I don't give up. And if you want to achieve a greater success and a deeper happiness through manifestation, you need to believe too.

When I first learned of the power of manifestation, I was intrigued but I was also sceptical. I wanted to test this new concept. I needed proof, so I started working on very small manifestation projects. I was challenging the Universe.

'Okay then, show me what you've got!' I said.

Now I'm not going to lie; there were occasions when my manifestation projects didn't seem to work. And there were times when I doubted myself and I became confused and overwhelmed and it all became too hard. Ultimately, it was my capacity to believe that got me over the line. It's what kept me going and encouraged me to keep persisting.

When I put my heart and soul into a manifestation project, I saw incredible and dramatic results. And when I got my entire family involved in the manifestation, the results couldn't be denied.

Our five-month-old puppy one day figured out she could jump the temporary toddler gate blocking the doorway of our kitchen. This gate was in place to stop her from getting into the hallway and down to the bedrooms and the rest of the house, where she could get in all sorts of mischief. She had access to the kitchen via a doggy door installed in our back door.

We were happy with her in the kitchen because it was solid flooring, but not happy with her roaming through the rest of the house. The gate jumping became a real problem, because once she realised she could do it, there was no stopping her. Or so we thought. Manifestation was a new concept to me then, so I decided to put this theory to the test.

I told my family of my idea and they were keen to join in. We dedicated a lot of our thoughts (and therefore, our energy) to our puppy staying in the kitchen where she was meant to be. We took our focus away from the gate and from the rest of the house, because we didn't want to draw attention to the things we wanted her to avoid. Our full focus went to a visual image of her happily residing in the kitchen and the backyard, where she was meant to be. And it worked.

Within a few short days, she had stopped jumping the gate. We made a point to do no extra training or techniques with her, so we could be certain the manifestation was the only variable that had changed during that time. There were no changes to her routine. She very quickly lost interest in jumping the gate and was happy with access to only the kitchen and the backyard. Coincidence? Perhaps. But I believe that our manifestation work created her change in behaviour.

This wasn't an isolated event. I have used manifestation for many things in the past few years, and it has worked. Sometimes the results were almost instant. Sometimes, it was a waiting game. Other times, it didn't work at all. Manifestations can't be guaranteed to work one hundred percent of the time, but despite this I still believe the evidence is crystal clear. My belief is, if what you are manifesting doesn't eventuate, it wasn't the best thing for you. Chances are, something else totally amazing has instead come your way!

Manifestations give us hope, therefore they give us strength and drive. And anything that influences your life in this positive way is a good thing! Could they be false hopes? I don't think there is such a thing as false hope. I believe that hope is simply, hope. After all, how can the act of wishing for something to happen be false? Essentially, that is what hope is; wishing for something that hasn't yet eventuated.

Forget about the end result for a moment; whether your manifestation works or not is irrelevant when you are in the midst of hope. When you are being enveloped in a sense of hope, it is very real and tangible – the comfort and strength this brings you is definitely not false. So then, does manifestation work? I believe it does.

Having a strong, intimate connection to your soul-self can help you with your manifestations. The more in sync you become with your soul energy, the easier it will be for you to figure out whether your dreams and goals are for your greatest good. You will feel it, deep within you. That beautiful *inner knowing*.

As you strive towards your own manifestations, and you feel like life keeps getting in the way or nothing seems to be going right, don't be disheartened. Return to love. Come back to your inner-self, your soul energy. Reassess. Recalibrate. Make a change. Visualise. Keep working hard. Get busy manifesting. You will get there! Just don't make that end goal the be-all and end-all of your existence. You must enjoy the ride! This is what living is all about – soaking up all the action along the way. Be in the moment as you encounter all experiences, whether they are phenomenal, life-changing experiences or subtle little ones. Live and love and learn through it all.

PART IV

COMING FULL CIRCLE

21

YOUR SOUL SPEAKS

'Pause, and listen.'

Have you ever been thinking of someone and your phone rings? You answer the call and on the other end of the line is that very same person you were just thinking of?

Have you ever experienced déjà vu? When you find yourself in a place or in a conversation that feels overwhelmingly familiar, despite never having been there, or having that conversation before?

Have you ever had random ideas pop into your head from seemingly nowhere, and when you act on them, things seem to work out beautifully?

These magical moments are to be treasured, and let me tell you why! Because in these fleeting moments your mind, body and soul are all working together in harmony. In the blink of an eye, with your entire being in a state of equilibrium, you hear the messages. You see the visions.

Cast your mind back to the introduction of this book. To a very young me, in the car on the way to my aunty and uncle's house, having a surreal experience I couldn't explain. It has taken me thirty five years to truly understand and appreciate the depth of that experience.

I was experiencing déjà vu, because my soul was remembering. Although I physically had never been to this place before, my soul had. My soul knew this place, and it was connecting. I remember feeling a little sleepy travelling in the back of the car, so I was extremely relaxed and uninhibited by thoughts or worries at the time; an ideal state to be in, to connect with the soul-self.

And would you believe, in my late thirties, my husband and I bought a house on this very road! As an adult, driving along that same road, although the landscape had changed significantly by means of many more houses and manicured parklands, I could recall *exactly* how I felt driving along this road all those years ago. I could feel the same energetic connections to this place. We didn't last long living in that house because the energy of the area was too much for me to bear, long term.

My soul has walked that land before, in another time. But that time has long gone. My energy was no longer needed there. During meditations, I have relived the ceremonies of local tribespeople taking place on that land. At other times, often in my dreams, I could see and sense the land of this place crying out in need of healing.

I now know that my soul has a very strong bond with that place; how extraordinary that my six-year-old self felt this bond. This gift we are all blessed with – the gift of being able to see, smell, hear, taste, feel, *know* energy, is a wonderous thing.

I listen to people sharing stories through everyday conversation, of moments of connectedness and synchronicity. Moments of energetic and spiritual communication, and these people haven't realised what has actually taken place in that moment!

Have you ever been walking past a building and you felt the overwhelming urge to go inside the building? That is your soul speaking. Your energy has connected with the energy of something or someone in that building and it is pulling you towards them.

Have you ever blurted out an observation about someone, only for them to seem stunned and suspicious because you were bang on the money and neither of you know why? Have you ever had a dream about being in a certain place you have never been before and this experience has, down the track, come true?

Have you ever looked back on the aftermath of a difficult situation and realised you had an inner knowing all along of what you needed to do, yet you were too afraid to trust yourself? *It is now time to trust yourself.*

Take your gift with both hands and love it with all your heart. Nurture it. Offer it patience and compassion. Learn to recognise the little signs and subtle messages that are all around you and *inside* you!

Your soul is constantly communicating with your body and your mind, such as those random ideas that, when followed through, bring unexpected joy. Your soul is intricately connected to all the other energies and to other souls around you, such as the person who rings you just as you were thinking of them.

Pause, and listen. Hear the whisperings of your soul, and let it lead you to a life of great happiness. You deserve a life full of laughter and fun and incredible experiences to blow your mind.

22

THE EVERYDAY YOU

'Always be true to yourself.'

In the beginning, it was vital that I dedicated as much time and energy as possible to my spiritual journey. The health of my entire being demanded it. It was all I ever thought about. I let spirituality and other-worldly concepts swallow me whole. Through this immersion, I found a happiness and love for myself and for everything and everyone that exceeded my wildest dreams; who knew life could be this good!

However, as time went on and my healing journey progressed, I reached a point when I realised I couldn't maintain that previous state of immersion. I had lost myself (and not in a good way).

Let me explain.

As I ventured on through my spiritual awakening, I lost sight of who I really wanted to be. I immersed myself so deeply in spirituality and spiritual practices that I forgot about all the other things in life that bring me joy and are important to me. You know, eighties pop music, sci-fi movies, vodkas and dancing, badminton, laughing at naughty jokes, cards nights. All these things make me who I am – not just spirituality.

For a while, I was trying so hard to fit in with the spiritual community, talking the talk and dressing a certain way. It felt so *wrong*, yet I couldn't work out why because I knew I wanted and *needed* to embrace my spiritual journey.

Now I realise that sometimes I want to dress and talk like a spiritual goddess, but most of the time I just want to be plain old me. Sometimes I wear flowy, flowery dresses and drape crystals around my neck, but most of the time I wear jeans or trackpants and a comfy t-shirt. Sometimes I can talk all day about spirits and energy and sometimes, all I want to do is spend a day talking about trashy television shows and eating way too much chocolate.

You may be destined to become a completely new you, or you may just need to integrate a few spiritual or self-care practices into your everyday life to enhance who you already are. I guess what I'm trying to say is, always be true to yourself.

If you don't want to throw yourself wholeheartedly into becoming a deeply spiritual person, then don't! If all you learn after reading this book is to meditate occasionally and this brings you huge levels of happiness, fantastic!

If all the spiritual talk makes you feel uneasy right now, but all the other self-care tips resonate and end up transforming your life, wonderful! Or perhaps you embrace every element of this book and you find a deep inner peace and self-love you never realised you were capable of. Everyone's journey is different. We are all here to achieve different levels of consciousness and learn different things.

Some people, after a spiritual awakening, may choose to sell everything so they can move to the bush, live off the land and fully immerse themselves in sacred spiritual practices. Other people will simply choose to put more effort into being a little kinder to themselves and to others as they go about their day. You are who you are. No judgement. Just acceptance. We are all entitled to feel happiness, love and a sense of connectedness to ourselves and to others.

I caught up with a dear friend recently who is struggling to feel spiritually connected and is putting a lot of pressure on herself and feeling a whole lot of guilt for not being spiritual enough. She wanted to know exactly what I did from the moment I woke each morning, to when I fell asleep at night. She assumed I would have a deeply sacred and spiritual morning ritual, that I eat wholesome organic food all the time, and that I spend all day helping and healing others.

She thought that because I am a healer with some incredible spiritual gifts and because of the work I do and because of how happy I am, this is who I would be in my down time. She was trying to turn herself into this *perfect spiritual being* and was burning herself out in the process. This idealism of spirituality was getting in the way of her realising her own, authentic journey.

So many people I talk to feel this same way. It's time to flip this unsustainable pursuit of perfection on its head. Let's keep it real.

My morning alarm goes off, I hit snooze a bunch of times, I drag myself out of bed and into the shower. If I'm feeling tired, I will do a quick energy cleanse while standing under the running water, but usually it's a quick rinse and then out, dressed, make kids' lunches, get them off to school, grab a quick bite to eat, then I get myself off to my healing room. I might see one or two clients during the day, run a meditation class for an hour, then go to the supermarket to get dinner, pick up the kids from school and head home.

I then might spend an hour or so doing administrative and promotional work for my business and for my husband's business, then I'll crash on the lounge with a cup of tea and a sweet treat, watch a couple of hours of my favourite television shows with my husband or I'll read a good book, do a puzzle or play with the dogs.

Usually I'll get a load of washing on and hung out ready for the next day, and then it's bedtime.

Here is how I weave the spiritual into my everyday: I protect my energy throughout the day, if I feel like I need it. This has become second nature to me and it will to you, too, with practise. I have brief conversations with my own soul and with other souls throughout the day; sometimes there are some strong and powerful connections, but mostly, it's seeing and feeling and acknowledging subtle little signs and messages that are all around me. I make time to catch up with friends and family I'm feeling drawn to at the time; sometimes it's friends from my spiritual circles, other times it's old friends from my childhood or sporting groups I've been in over the years, or various family members. I also make time to be by myself as often as I need to. Knowing I have this eclectic mix of personalities and energy close by is vital for balancing my overall wellbeing.

Every evening, when I'm laying in bed and ready for sleep, I will charge myself with universal life force energy until I can feel it flowing through my body. I'll then unclench my jaw and relax my tongue in my mouth and focus on my breathing. This evening routine will send me off to sleep within minutes, if not seconds. The healing energy then flows through me while I sleep, for as long as it is needed.

If I'm having a tough day or I'm feeling tired or emotional or I'm dealing with some major life events, then I'll go to extra lengths to incorporate more spiritual self-care into my day. It's knowing these techniques and having this knowledge on hand for whenever it is needed, that matters. I seek the services of other local healers, so I can surrender to my own healing experiences every couple of months in the care of someone else. I also try and regularly attend spiritual workshops or retreats at least a couple of times a year.

But for the most part I'm a regular, everyday person who just happens to embrace energy and spirituality and who knows some really handy tools and techniques that, over the years, have been invaluable to my health, happiness and overall wellbeing.

This is what you, too, can do for yourself. So you see, there is no such thing as a perfect life; there is no one-size-fits-all mould for happiness and spirituality. Yes, there will be times when you need to throw yourself into the deep end of spirituality, but there will also be times when you can paddle in the shallows. Take what you have learned from this book, no matter how big or small, and let this knowledge weave its way into your life.

Living a soulful, happy and fulfilling life should be fun. Go and grab that happiness with both hands, in whatever capacity you can!

23

GUIDANCE FROM SPIRIT

'These incredible messages from Spirit are just for you.'

I would like to invite you to browse through the following pages. Here, you will discover gifts of wisdom, encouragement, strength and hope delivered through me, from Spirit. Take your time.

Feel the love beaming from the pages; stretching its arms out wide to embrace you. These incredible messages from Spirit are just for you; to guide you, to help you heal, to encourage you, to give you strength, to shift your perspective, to remind you that *you* matter, always.

These words, forming the foundations of these messages and ultimately, the foundations of this book, flowed from me during times of channelling Spirit with the intent of sharing their message with the world. With you.

Return to these messages as often as you need; they are forever here for you.

STAND TALL

Know this: you are courageous, strong, confident. You are a warrior!

Feel these powerful energies rise within you, then stand tall.

Hold your head up.
Release any shame.
Take a deep breath in.
Let go of any fear.

In this moment, nothing else matters!

Pause, breathe. Stand tall and proud.

Eyes up, chest forward, shoulders down.

Step into this next moment of your future with love in your heart and strength in your soul.

You got this.

YOU ARE BLESSED

Whether you are happy, or hurting.
In love, or still searching.
Making millions, or scratching for a dollar.

Whatever is happening to you right now, it is important to remind yourself that you are blessed.

If life is amazing, stay humble and thankful.
If life is hard, stay positive and hopeful.

Everything, absolutely everything, is temporary. The good, the not so good, and everything in between.

Life is a constant flow of change and growth and lessons.

This is *your* journey, and it is a blessing.

Please know: *you* are a blessing.

EVERY NOW AND THEN, YOU MUST ALLOW YOURSELF TO SIMPLY DRIFT

Learning and healing and exploring and living are all extremely important. Crucial, in fact. However there are times when you need to stop.

To float atop the ocean of Universal energy that surrounds us all.
To let the gentle pull of the current take you where you need to go.

Simply drift. No effort, no anything, just being.

You owe yourself this much.

You give yourself permission to stop.

You acknowledge that drifting is a crucial part of this journey you are on.

Find your ocean, and surrender.

Happy drifting, beautiful soul!

Guidance from Spirit

The following message is intended for everyone – whether you are fit, healthy, blissfully happy, or sick, depressed, worn out, struggling with disease and everything in between. This message is for all of you…

LOVE ALL OF YOURSELF, FLAWS AND ALL. LOVE YOUR ENTIRE BEING JUST AS IT IS RIGHT NOW

(Picture arms madly swinging around in the air, to emphasise the point.)

You are perfect, just as you are. Your flaws are a part of you; embrace them and love all of you. ALL OF YOU!! *Warts, and all.*

Those parts of you that are sick, diseased, unhappy – they need your love the most. Those specific cells, that energy, desperately needs your love.

love
love
love
love
love

SLOW DOWN. STEP BACK. ALLOW YOURSELF TIME TO REGROUP, TO FIND PERSPECTIVE

Life is not a race.

The world won't fall apart if you take a minute, an hour, a day to step back and regroup.

Escape to nature, where you can reconnect with that all-important Earth energy.

You can't give others the love and attention they need, if you are racing through time and never stopping to breathe and to just BE.

Give yourself permission to stop.

Reflect. Rest. Heal.

FIND YOUR PEACE

Allow P E A C E to trickle through you right now, in this moment, caressing your body, mind and soul.

Let peace seep out of your pores, so others may feel it too.

Let it flow through you every second of every day.

Feel content, knowing you may return to this internal river of solace anytime, anywhere.

Dig deep, until you find your vein of inner-peace.

Tap into it.

Use it.

Feel it.

Trust it!

Here is a little energetic exercise channelled from Spirit,
to bring some light and grace to your day.

IMAGINE THIS…

The sun is shining. Feel the sun's rays on your bare skin.
Pause, and feel the warmth.

The sky is an endless blue expanse above you.
Pause, and lose yourself in the vastness.

You see a small, white bird in the distance, about to take flight.
See the bird's wings unfold and stretch.
See the bird's feet leave the ground.
Watch, as it glides effortlessly through the sky.

Pause, and feel the grace of flight.
Feel the weightlessness consume you.

You are one with the bird.
Flying in the sky.
No thoughts.
No worries.
No boundaries.

Free.

RE-IGNITE YOUR INNER FIRE!

No more plodding along doing things you *sort of* enjoy.

Do more of what you are truly passionate about.

There is a stunning sunrise on the way for you; it is just around the corner, but you need to stoke your inner fire first.

Even if you can just stir the embers inside you, that is still a great step forward! The fire will soon follow.

Build your fire in preparation for your sunrise that you are about to witness.

Because this sunrise is not something you are going to want to miss!

It is going to be magnificent.

YOUR EFFORTS CONTRIBUTE TO YOUR HAPPINESS!

Best friends, husbands, wives, life partners, parents, siblings, yoga instructors, personal and life coaches, healers, psychics, teachers and mentors can and do help you. But what are you doing to help yourself?

Stop placing the responsibility of your happiness solely in the hands of other people. It is your responsibility.

So, what *can* you do to help yourself?

This is the question you need to keep asking yourself, and don't stop asking until you have an answer.

Take back your power!

Let others help, guide and love you, but ultimately *you* must put the effort in and get busy bringing more happiness into your life.

YOUR SOUL IS STIRRING

There are feelings deep within you, being aroused.

If those feelings feel negative, allow them to rise to the surface — feel them with every inch of your body and soul, thank them, then let them go.

Imagine these feelings as a physical form — see it in your mind's eye, and watch as it leaves your body. Perhaps you will see black smoke or dust.

Whatever you see, is right for you. Trust it.

If those feelings feel positive and good, embrace them with open arms!

Let them explode from within you!

Let them overcome you!

Let your *inner light* shine.

This is your time.

NATURE IS POWERFUL AND BEAUTIFUL

Nature is powerful and beautiful.

And guess what?

You are nature.

You are part of Mother Earth.

You are part of the intricate web of energy connecting the Universe.

Therefore, *you* are powerful and beautiful.

THE POINT TO LIFE, IS HAPPINESS!

~~~~ ~~~~

Welcome happiness into your life with open arms!

Remind yourself, all the time, of what makes you happy!

Do something every single day that brings you joy!

Life isn't meant to be mundane, and it doesn't have to be that way!

Get busy bringing happiness back into your life!

LOOK TO THE SKY

Whenever life gets you down, look to the sky.

Star gaze, or lay and watch the daytime clouds roll by.

This act of stillness, of connecting with the Greater Universe, will soothe your soul and hush your mind.

A wave of peace will wash over you, as your soul energy consciously connects to the energy and wonder of the Universe.

YOUR JOURNEY IS JUST AS IMPORTANT AS YOUR DESTINATION. ENJOY THE RIDE

The destination is important.

But always remember, the journey is also important.

For without the journey, there can be no destination.

Without the journey, there can be no lessons.

Without the journey, there can be no change.

When you feel that life is getting you down because you can never get to where you are going… stop.

Forget about the destination, just for a little while.

Life is fun! Living is fun!

Find the joy in living again, so you can enjoy the ride.

CHANGE IS BEAUTIFUL

Transformation.

Evolution.

Growth.

It is necessary and inevitable.

Embrace it, don't be afraid.

Know that as things are falling apart, they are making way for bigger and better things.

Chaos is temporary.

Happiness and love are eternal.

THE POSSIBILITIES IN LIFE ARE ENDLESS, IF YOU OPEN YOURSELF UP TO THEM

Don't ever discount anything, even if it seems completely out of reach.

Possibilities are what dreams are made of and dreams can easily (and often do) become realities.

Keep dreaming.

Stay hopeful.

Be positive.

Show gratitude.

Possibilities are everywhere, just waiting for the right moment to present themselves.

YOUR BODY IS DESERVING OF YOUR UNCONDITIONAL LOVE

Your body is the vessel that holds your soul, and it has an incredibly huge job to do!

Sometimes, it struggles and becomes weak or injured. All the more reason to love it unconditionally.

When a friend is sad or sick, you send them love without thinking twice. Think of your body as your best friend! Nurture it. Love it. Be kind and patient with it. And listen to its subtle little messages, because it is always communicating with you.

Is there something about your body that you don't like, are ashamed of, or wish you could change? Try focusing on that body part instead of glancing past it, like you usually do. Look at it with a sense of intrigue and curiosity.

Look at it with new, fresh eyes. Really study it.

Push past the embarrassment or hatred that you may perhaps usually feel.
Find the beauty in it, because it is there!

Stay with it, until your perception begins to change for the better, just a little bit.

Then next time stay with it even longer. Your body will respond!

It is your body, your temple.

Love it unconditionally, and it will respond to that love.

Body and soul, working as one.
A true and fierce force of nature you will then be!

BEAUTY IS IN THE EYE OF THE BEHOLDER

You decide what you consider to be beautiful. Please, open your eyes and your heart a little wider.

Beauty is everywhere. Beauty is right in front of you, beauty is inside you; it is all around you.

The more beauty you behold, the more beauty beholds you.

Be a seeker.

Go and find beauty in the little things and see how much happiness it brings you.

LIGHT THE WAY

Be brave enough to walk your path, without the fear of judgement or criticism from others.

Shoulders back, head up; you are you, and you are proud.

If you worry about not fitting in, you can't ever be true to yourself. You can't ever be your organic, beautiful self.

Be brave!

Light the way.

Others will respect you and love you and those who don't, aren't destined to be in your life for much longer.

You will inspire others to be brave.

Shine bright, beautiful soul!

Light the way.

INDEX

Abhyanga Massage 208-211
Aboriginal Healing 150-156
Abundance
- affirmations on 102, 232
- manifestation of 229-232

Acupressure
- for muscle pain 178-179
- on feet 179

Acupuncture 176-180
Affirmations 100-102, 171, 217-218
Allergies
- of food 190
- The Food Disasters 190-192

Anger
- Love & Anger/Conflict 80-84
- acupuncture for 177

Aura 45-47
Autoimmune Disease 189
Autosuggestion 215-218
Ayurveda
- Abhyanga 208-211
- massage 209-210

Belinda's Story 90-93

Bowen Therapy
- My Story 15

Chakras 47-49, 212
Children
- auras 45-46
- dream catchers / room cleanse 223-224
- food 194-196
- intuition 67
- meditation in schools 139
- protective bubble 184
- sensing souls 44-45
- shower cleanse 182
- The Sway Test 65-67

Cleanse Energy
- around you 222-224
- in you 182-183
- of crystals 162
- shower cleanse exercise 182

Colours
- of auras 45-46
- of chakras 48-49

Communication
- in relationships 103
- of deceased souls 42-44, 58-59
- of spiritual energy 54-56
- pendulums 64-65
- The Sway Test 65-67
- Yes/No Test 61-63

Conflict
- Lessons: Navigating Through the Speedbumps (chapter) 108-114
- Love and Anger/Conflict 80-84

Crystals
- healing with 160-162
- pendulums 64-65

Death
- of Jo's father 31-32
- Spiritual Energy and Death 57-60

Déjà vu 237-238
Dream Catcher 223-224
Dreamtime
- Aboriginal healing 150-156

Drumming 22

Ear Massage 211-212
Earthing 180-182
- Earthing visualisation exercise 181

Ego
- Ego (chapter) 85-88
- Jo's ego 94

Emotions
- as energy 55, 57, 77
- crystals arousing 161
- human experience 107, 113
- qi (Traditional Chinese Medicine) 176-177
- sacral chakra 48
- tapping 170-176

Exercise
- for the mind 203
- Intuition and a Happy Body 200-203
- Traditional Chinese Medicine 177

Five Senses
- communication of energy 55
- stimulate the 224-225

Float Therapy 219
Food Intolerances 188-189
Foot Massage 179, 211-212

Gemstones
- healing with 160-163
- pendulums 64-65

Ghosts
- encounters with 43-45

God 51
Grounding 180-182
- Earthing visualisation exercise 181

Guardian Angels 42-43, 45
Gut Health 192-193

Hawaiian Massage 207

Herbs 198-199
Hope 101, 234
Hypnotherapy 213-215, 218

Intolerances 188

Journaling 165, 203
Joy List 84

Kahuna Massage 207

Law of Attraction 57
'Love Thyself' 167

Manifestation
 - Manifestation of Your Dreams (chapter) 227-234
 - positive affirmations 100-102
 - vision boards 95-99
Mantra, The 'I Love Me' 75
Meridians 171, 176, 212
Mindfulness 204-205
Money
 - lessons on 229-232
 - more of 86
 - reduce debt and increase cash flow 103
Music 73, 84, 142-143, 153, 204, 222, 224

On Country Healing 152
Oracle Cards 22

Pendulum 64-65
Positive Affirmations 100-102, 171, 217-218, 227
Protect Energy 183-185
 - Bubble machine exercise 184
Psychic Abilities
 - Jo's healings and 35-36
 - definition of 55
 - ego affecting 86

Reiki
 - Jo's story 24-35
 - what is 146-150
 - paediatrician using 185-186
Relationships
 - toxic 82-83
 - communication within 103
 - failing unnecessarily 104
 - lessons from 112
 - healing 144, 165
 - letting go of 221

Shamanic Healing 156-160
Sound Healing
 - with mindfulness 204
 - for space clearing 222

- The Five Senses 224
Spirit Guides 42-43
Spirits 42-45
Stories 39
Strengthen Energy 183
Sway Test, The 65-67

Tapping 170-176
Thoughts
- communication of spiritual energy using 54-56
- sharing the love with 79
- during anger/conflict 80-81
Traditional Chinese Medicine
- acupuncture 176-180

Vibrations
- high vibrations 57
- of crystals 160-161
- through drumming 22
Vision Board 95-99
Visualisation Techniques
- for cleansing energy 182
- for grounding 181
- for protecting energy 184
- to charge pendulum 64
- to cleanse crystals 162
- to enhance bath time 219

Words, Healing Power of 166-167

Yes / No Test 61-63

⋘ HELPFUL RESOURCES ⋙

These documentaries and books changed my life in those first few years of learning about energy and Spirit and other-worldly concepts. Not all of them are spiritual, but they were all pivotal in my journey to this point.

DOCUMENTARIES
The Grounded, Steve Kroschel, earthing.
Heal, Kelly Noonan, healing.
The Secret, Drew Heriot (also a book, author Rhonda Byrne), The Law of Attraction.
The Story of God with Morgan Freeman, National Geographic, the meaning of life, and *God* in different cultures.
The Sacred Science, Nicholas J Polizzi, healing.

BOOKS
Perfect Health, Deepak Chopra, self-help, Ayurvedic Medicine.
Light is the New Black: A Guide to Answering Your Soul's Callings and Working Your Light, Rebecca Campbell, self-help, following your path.
Rosemary Gladstar's Herbal Recipes for Vibrant Health, Rosemary Gladstar, reference, easy herbal recipes and tips.
The Crystal Bible Volume 1, Judy Hall, reference, a detailed A-Z on crystals and gemstones. (Volumes 2 and 3 also available.)
The Barefoot Investor: The Only Money Guide You'll Ever Need, Scott Pape, reference, personal money management.

Energy Speaks: Messages from Spirit on Living, Loving, and Awakening, Lee Harris, self-help, channelled Spirit messages.
Nourishing Traditions, Sally Fallon, cookbook/reference, ancestral cooking.

There are honest and hard-working healers and holistic health professionals all over this beautiful planet of ours. Go out and find them! Ask for recommendations from friends, acquaintances and family. Reach out to your local community for help in finding these incredible, kind-hearted souls. Do some online research. Trust your intuition to lead you to the right people at the right time in your life.

WITH DEEPEST GRATITUDE

Thank you to my family for listening to my ramblings, tolerating the hours on end of writing and researching, and for loving me for who I am. We make a pretty awesome team, and I love you all endlessly.

To all the healers and therapists who generously donated their knowledge and time for my research, you are all incredible!

And to everyone who supports my little energy healing business; all clients and colleagues and acquaintances, without you, I wouldn't be doing what I am doing.

Gratitude to Shirley, Mel, AJ, Trish, Lynda and Nicholas for being so generous and inspiring.

An extra-special thank you to The Ladybirds; without you, I wouldn't have made it this far.

And finally, thank you to Spirit and the Universe for all the teachings, insights, and love.

A NOTE ON THE AUTHOR

Jo Worsfold is a Tasmanian author on a mission. Tasmania is a little island off the south coast of the Australian mainland, known by the locals as The Apple Isle. This has been Jo's home for most of her life and she loves living here with her mechanic husband, their two highly intuitive children and two totally gorgeous Labradoodles.

What is Jo's mission? To saturate the whole world with love and kindness, of course! Jo is achieving this by combining her passion for writing with her healing gift and her down to earth nature. The result: hippy books that make sense.

Jo is a nature-loving spiritualist who adores all kinds of music from Whitney Houston to Hilltop Hoods. She also loves dabbling in nature photography, sipping on vodka lime sodas or even better, a good cup of tea. She's always up for a hit at social badminton and she has a very real crush on love-struck vampires.

⋘ KEEP IN TOUCH ⋙

Get all the latest news

from

JO WORSFOLD

www.lumanova.com.au

Like Jo on Facebook
/lumanovaoz

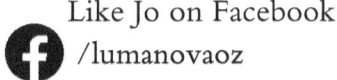
Follow Jo on Instagram
/lumanova_healer

www.ingramcontent.com/pod-product-compliance
Lightning Source LLC
Chambersburg PA
CBHW032029290426
44110CB00012B/734